THE KINNAKEETER

SIR WALTER RALEIGH

The Queen of England gave patents to Sir Walter Raleigh to plant colonies in the New World. The first voyage made to the New World under the direction of Sir Walter Raleigh was under the command of Captains Philip Amadas and Arthur Barlowe in 1584. The second voyage was under the command of Sir Richard Grenville in 1585. The third voyage was made by Sir Richard Grenville and was sent for the relief of the colony planted in Virginia. The fourth voyage was made under the command of John White. This was a new colony of one hundred and fifty men. Raleigh, in his attempt to make a permanent settlement, was being unsuccessful but he persevered doggedly in his attempts. The fifth voyage was under the command of John White, but he spent most of his time pirating the Spanish ships laden with gold from South America and his colony perished.

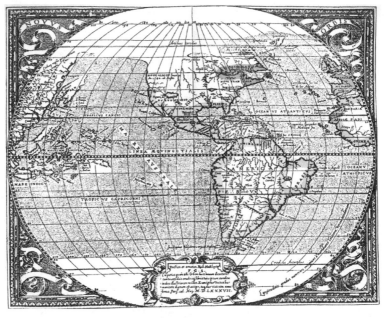

MAP OF THE NEW WORLD

First map made of the New World.
The year of our Lord 1587.

THE KINNAKEETER

SECOND EDITION

Illustrated

Charles T. Williams II

CHAPEL HILL

FULL-SERVICE   BOOK-MAKERS
ESTD.   1996

PRESS

About the cover image: The first Pirate's Jamboree was held at the Cape Hatteras Lighthouse on April 29, 1955. The event included a fish fry near the lighthouse in Buxton. Many thanks to John Havel for locating this image and providing it for use on the cover.

Portrait of Sir Walter Raleigh reprinted courtesy of the National Portrait Gallery Picture Library, London

Map of the New World and The First Lords Proprietors' Map of Carolina reprinted courtesy of the Louis Round Wilson Special Collections Library, The University of North Carolina at Chapel Hill.

ISBN 978-1-59715-125-2
Library of Congress Catalog Number 2015957524

First Printing
Printed in the United States of America

This book is dedicated to the Kinnakeeter, my people, Mrs. Margaret Price, for Civil War history and traditions, Rev. A.W. Price for authentic and historical traditions, Charles Williams I, my father, for the wealth of constant instruction and teaching that he has imparted to me.

CONTENTS

LIST OF ILLUSTRATIONS

INTRODUCTION

In this affectionate and carefully documented "Portrait of the Kinnakeeter," Charles T. Williams II, a Kinnakeeter himself, introduces us to a remarkable breed of American who, while friendly and Christian (in the highest sense of that ill-used term), is jealously protective of his independence. A search of the dictionary or the gazetteer will not reveal the word itself, but there is a word, *kinnikinnick*, which is derived from an Algonquian word which means "that which is mixed." And so, ages before Israel Zangwill thought of America as a "melting pot," the Indians of Hatteras Island and thereabouts had a word for it. And the mixture, as Mr. Williams tells us, began with shipwrecked sailors, victims of the treacherous waters of the "graveyard of the Atlantic," and their hospitable Algonquian Indian rescuers, way back in the 1500s.

This little taste of history should send us looking for further information on the efforts at colonization by Sir Walter Raleigh and others, especially theories on the "Lost Colony," but Mr. Williams's chief concern is with today's Kinnakeeter.

Naturally, the chief occupations are concerned with the sea. From the earliest days, the Kinnakeeter was aware of the riches to be wrested from the waters—not only from the abundant and varied fish to be netted or hooked but also from salvaged vessels, hopefully after the human cargo had been, in most cases, heroically rescued at the risk of the Kinnakeeters' lives. In more recent times, a chief support of the area has been employment by the United States Coast Guard, which found a rich pool of recruits among the veterans of the earlier Lifesaving Service. In the 1800s, a man with the unlikely name of Pharoah Farrow made a fortune in timber on the islands—a fortune, incidentally, reputed to be buried somewhere. Mr. Williams tells a charming story of how God helped the Kinnakeeters to build a church by seeding the mudflats with oysters—which brought premium prices on the mainland.

Mr. Williams tells us about the natural resources, especially the wild waterfowl that nest there. He tells about the church, education, the recreation—but the proudest thing is the community spirit, a resource sorely needed in this tired world.

FOREWORD

A few years after *The Kinnakeeter* was published in 1975, a sign on a fish house at the village harbor caught my eye. The sign was hand-painted, partially in block letters and partially in a soft, flowing script that stood apart from the weathered siding on the building, the workboats docked there, and the fishermen unloading their catch.

The sign said, "Avon Seafood, live hard crabs, clams and oysters, and maybe fish."

I was still a newcomer to the island and the inclusion of the word "maybe" on the sign puzzled me until I had lived here long enough to begin to understand the honest and absolute respect Kinnakeeters have for the vagaries of the sea.

Few modern communities share the deep reverence Kinnakeet holds for the gifts and blessings that come from the sea or share such a rich seafaring history.

The Kinnakeeter captures that history in stories about the schooners and other vessels that set sail from the village, carrying oysters, fish, mail, and passengers to mainland towns, in stories about shipwrecks, and in stories about the local men who served at the Coast Guard stations.

The sea not only sustained trade and commerce but shaped other parts of village life. Sailboats brought friends from other Outer Banks communities to religious camp meetings on the Pamlico shoreline, and sail skiff racing drew large numbers of spectators.

When Buxton Village Books owner Gee Gee Rosell told me that she was working with Chapel Hill Press on clearing the way for *The Kinnakeeter* to be reprinted, I was excited but not terribly surprised. Gee Gee's commitment to helping maintain the authentic Hatteras Island culture is obvious the moment you walk into her store and Chapel Hill Press has long helped individuals share stories that deepen our collective appreciation of unique cultures and places.

When Gee Gee asked me to write an introduction for the reprinting, I felt honored to participate in a small way in making this book available to not only a new generation of Kinnakeeters but to all the people who love Hatteras Island.

For the past several years, I've been working on an Outer Banks oral history project called Coastal Voices. Older oral history interviews recorded on cassette tape have been digitized and a team of community volunteers are conducting new interviews.

Many of the narrators have been Kinnakeeters and they have shared stories replete with the same resourcefulness and resiliency evident in *The Kinnakeeter*.

Susan West
Buxton, North Carolina
November 2015

THE KINNAKEETER

Theodore de Bry Map

PORTRAIT OF THE KINNAKEETER

God, in evaluating His own portrait, said, "I am that I am. I am your Father, the God of Abraham, Isaac and Jacob. I am the Lord and there is none other beside me." Christ, in evaluating a descriptive portrait of himself, said, "I am the Way, the Truth, and the Life. I am the root and offspring of David, the bright and morning star." God called Cyrus, King of Persia, "My shepherd, my anointed;" that was God's description of King Cyrus' portrait.

All of God's created sentient beings have some characteristics that delineate a portrait of their being. In our portrayal of the Kinnakeeter, that is what we will try and endeavor to do. Nearly the entire population of Kinnakeet read the morning paper; they like company; fifty per cent meet friends weekly, seventy-five percent visit parents and kinsmen weekly. Television is popular; half of the population visits movies, also half of the population attends church services. They spend a lot of time at work, but more time at eating, caring for children. Women read more than men. Saturday night is the most popular night out; television has supplanted the radio to some extent. They are civic-minded to the best of their abilities and environment.

You can see him in the ancient days shipwrecked on the Kinnakeet beaches dejected, forlorn and homesick for his native land. You can see him becoming an honored member of

1

the tribe of friendly Indians, raising his children in a solitary beautiful paradise of God; catching fish, oysters, clams, and wild fowl; raising cattle, pigs, horses, and living a free life unlike any other people in the world. You can see him building his ships and becoming master of the inland waters of North Carolina. You can see him exchanging the products of the sea for the corn and potatoes of the mainland, erecting his windmills to grind his corn into meal for the sustenance of his body. You can hear him praising the Lord in the forest, on the beaches, in the little dilapidated village school building, in his neighbor's home, in the new Holy Temple of God that he has erected to the glory of his Maker. You can see him educating his children and making them honored and useful citizens of his state and nation. You can see him as the night watchman rescuing unfortunate humanity that are shipwrecked in raging seas, see him piloting them over the bar to a haven of safety, feeding their hungry bodies and dressing their wounds. You can see him with a drawn sword in defence of his country, swimming and diving through flaming waters in Pearl Harbor, landing on unfriendly shores fighting a desperate enemy in mud and mire of disease-infected jungles at Guadalcanal, Saipan and fighting hand-to-hand on the islands of the South Pacific and Central Pacific, weak and staggering on the death march of Bataan, languishing in Japanese prisons and dying from starvation where his cries are not heard and help never comes, where death is a pleasant relief.

This entire book is a fitting portrait of the Kinnakeeter.

Without dissent or acrimony, with love to all humanity and malice toward none, a nobler race of people never lived than the Kinnakeeter.

God bless you, with my love.

CHARLES T. WILLIAMS II

ON THE WINGS OF THE EAST WIND

The nucleus of birth of the race of the Kinnakeeter was borne on the wings of an East wind from the plains of Shinar in Babylonia, which culminated in the discovery, exploration, and settlement of the New World, known as America, by amalgamation of shipwrecked sailors and Indians on Hatteras Island. The Chicamacomicoer, Kinnakeeter and Hatterasman, all have the same customs, culture and tribal traits of the Algonquin Indians. More particularly and directly I am devoting my book, THE KINNAKEETER to the Kinnakeeters.

God created the Heavens and the Earth and, in the Shekina of His Majesty, viewed the wonders of his handiwork and said, "It is good." Man, the prime object of his creation and the love of His heart and constant lover, companion in Eden, came in contact with the red dragon, the old devil and degraded himself and his descendants. He believed a big lie and, by a shameful fall from God's grace, alienated himself from God's presence. Sin began to reap its fearful toll, and wreaked upon man, death, shame, disease, and decadence from God. God placed His hand in the hand of His beloved son and with compassion and pity led him through the streets of Eden and unlocked the door of entrance to the world of sin, thorns and thistles, ruled and dominated by sinful, cruel evil spirits who exacted the last vestige of beauty and love from his nature and left him to kill and destroy one another in an orgy of blood, death, hate and selfishness and total destruction of

3

all that was good. Sin waxed to a great crescendo. Men became lovers of men and God repented that he had made man, who had degraded himself lower than beasts. The foundations of the physical world were broken up and the mystical Continent of Atlantis disappeared and sank into the bowels of the Earth and tidal waves of great proportions engulfed the Earth and all life perished except Noah and his family. Noah and his family enjoyed a population explosion, but for fear of another flood occurring they clung to the mountains.

God told them to leave their sanctuary and go out on the wings of the East wind, multiply and inhabit the earth. Westward they started and on the plains of Shinar in Babylonia they halted their march and started to build a tower that would reach into the heavens. God came down and visited His children to inspect their tower. God knew the fear that was ruling their hearts. Being one race and one language they could accomplish anything that they put their minds and hearts to do. God repainted their skins in many colors and hues, confounded their tongues and gave them new languages. The tower became a tower of babbling tongues, confusion ensued, hot tempers displayed and the dispersion of man over the face of the Earth began.

It is a legend of tradition that Noah became a yellow man—Mongolian—and traveled Eastward and founded the Chinese Empire. All the peoples of Asia and isles of the Far Eastern seas were mongoloid of various hues and tints, the more reddish-skinned traveled through Siberia, and crossed the Straits of Behring and inhabited America. Japhet was white Caucasian; he had seven sons. They inhabited all of Eastern Europe and Central Europe to the Atlantic Ocean. Ham was very dark in color, negroid, and inhabited the African continent. Shem was white Caucasian. He had five sons, they inhabited all the land from the Euphrates river to the Indian ocean and all the land bordering the Red Sea which comprises most of the Middle East. They were fortunate. This land was the paradise of God which contained the City of Eden.

On the wings of the East Wind, the star of empires,

civilization, inventions, technology, discovery, exploration and settlement moved westward. The Three Wise Men from the East followed the bright star in the skies on the wings of the East wind. It stopped over the cradle in Bethlehem where the Prince of Glory lay in swaddling clothes in a manger. From then on the star of Christianity winged its flight on the wings of the East wind and brought grace, love and hope of eternal life to man in the Western world.

In the ancient world brave men went down to the sea in ships. Phoenicia, a nation on the Mediterranean seacoast, because of its commercial greatness was called "the England of Antiquity." Its seaports of Tyre, Sidon, Gebal and Arvad were filled with ships and sailors. Her sailors were the best and most efficient in the world. They were masters of all the shipping on the Mediterranean Sea lanes. Her ships sailed west on the wings of the East wind and transported the lost tribe of the House of Israel, through the Straits of Gibraltar to the west coast of Europe, settling them in Spain, England, France and the Scandinavian countries.

King Solomon was the world's largest shipbuilding magnate of the ancient world. Solomon built a vast navy of ships in Ezion Geber which was beside Eloth on the shores of the Red Sea in the land of Edom. He employed Phoenician sailors to man his ships to go to Ophir to bring him gold and silver for his great temple. He sent them to India and they brought back spices, peacocks, apes and linen of pure silk.

Men continued to go down to sea in sailing ships. The star of wealth, silk, gold, silver and empire beckoned him to sail westward into the unknown, where possible disasters were lurking in every move, where vicious sea monsters, envisioned as red dragons of the deep with long tails that could reach to the top mast of their ships, entwined their tails around the top of the mast and dragged his ship down to a watery grave and devoured the crew. Or he would arrive at the rim of the earth and drop off into the dark abyss.

5

Christopher Columbus defied these weird, lurid tales of horror and defeat that developed in the minds of morbid moronic unlettered people. He spread his sails on three ships and on the wings of the East wind he sailed westward in search of a new route to India. On the 14 of August 1492 he arrived at San Salvador in the West Indies. He launched his yawl boat and went ashore. The first man that left his yawl was a Jew named Torres. The sailors prayed and thanked God for their success. Columbus was greeted by a new race of people and he called them Indians. This was the greatest maritime feat ever accomplished by man. This heroic feat of fortitude and determination ushered in to the world a new day.

The discovery of America, its subsequent exploration and settlement are man's greatest material achievements.

America is the finished product of men who went to sea on ships and sailed westward on the wings of the East wind.

Americans are restless. They are now sailing on the wings of an upward wind exploring the planetary system and subsequently will colonize the moon.

KINNAKEET—THE ATLANTIC PARADISE

The State of North Carolina, in its travelogue film entitled *North Carolina, The Goodliest Land*, is advertising the beautiful scenery and places of attraction of North Carolina to the tourists of all lands. In the part that I played representing Hatteras Island, I coined the phrase and referred to Hatteras Island as the "Hawaii of the Atlantic!" Charles Heatherly, Publication Editor, Travel and Promotion Division of the Department of Natural and Economic Resources said, "Personally I think that your voice referring to your area as the Hawaii of the Atlantic is one of the really touching parts of the film. We are real proud of the film and certainly appreciate your efforts to help tell the good story of North Carolina."

In this book I am describing Kinnakeet as the Paradise of the Atlantic, and telling the unique story of the proud Kinnakeeter.

On a dreadful fateful day in the Paradise of God in the Euphrates Valley God apportioned condemnation upon man, woman and Satan, and the earth was shorn of its beauty and grandeur. On this day God reserved Kinnakeet in its primitive beauty and innocence as the future home of his elect people —the Kinnakeeter.

Four hundred years ago the Kinnakeet Banks was an unspoiled virgin land, the Paradise of the Atlantic. Its flora and fauna, or physiographic conditions then prevailing, were of indescribable beauty and majestic grandeur. Its average width was six miles from the Atlantic Ocean to the Pamlico Sound. Its length about thirty-six miles.

It was forested by stately pines, beautiful holly, giant oaks, flowering dogwood and magnificent cedars, more beautiful than the famed cedars of Lebanon. The vegetation of this semi-tropical paradise covered the face of Kinnakeet from the Pamlico Sound to the Atlantic Ocean in massive profusion. Beautiful flowers of many varieties and variegated colors spread their sweet influences over the face of the land. Grape vines covered the top of the forest on the Atlantic Ocean side of the Kinnakeet Banks and were overhanging down into the ocean and bearing grapes in abundance, the sea surging into the vines, and the ocean running purple with grape juice.

Sailors on Spanish galleons passing the coast on their way to Europe laden with pirate loot were captivated by the fragrant smell and aroma of the honeysuckle, cape jasmine and perfume from wild flowers that was wafted out to sea.

The coastal region consisted of sandy ridges densely forested, averaging twenty feet in height all the way from Ocracoke to Nags Head. So dense was the vegetation that one could travel on Indian trails within fifty feet of the ocean and never see the sea.

This was the Paradise of the Atlantic, God's earthly heaven inhabited by the Indians known as the Kinnakeet tribe.

FIRST SETTLERS

In 1585, a band of 108 men sailed from England sent by Sir Walter Raleigh to settle in the new region, then known as Virginia. This was a great territory in North America extending from the present state of Pennsylvania through North and South Carolina. The colonists who settled on Roanoke Island had hard times; they were surrounded by the unfriendly Indians and their supply of food was short. Within a year the men sailed back to England on the ships of Sir Francis Drake. In 1587, Raleigh recruited a group of 150 settlers for the colony in Virginia. John White, who led the group, was instructed to move the settlement from Roanoke Island to the shores of Chesapeake Bay, but the sailors refused to carry the colonists farther than Roanoke; the group was forced to land. Not one of the fifteen men who had remained the year before was found alive.

On August 18th, 27 days after the colonists landed a baby girl was born. She was the granddaughter of John White and the first English child born on the American continent. She was named Virginia Dare.

White returned to England for greatly needed supplies, but was not able to come back to America until 1590. When he landed at the site of the English Colony on Roanoke Island he found no trace of the colony, except the word "Croatan," which was carved on a tree. White had his fleet anchored in Shallow Bag Bay, which was then the harbor of Manteo, N.

C. A northeast storm of great intensity arose and for the safety of his ships he ordered his ship commanders to secure everything on deck, reef their sails, go to sea, and ride out the storm.

His Majesty's Ship, *John Evangelist*, with her sails torn to shreds, was unable to maneuver and could no longer ride out the storm and had no recourse but to scud before the wind in a southerly direction. Upon her arrival at the Indian village of Kinnakeet, the captain had to beach his ship. Her captain was a man named Caleb Williams, an Englishman; her mate was Elijah Meekins, and her cook was David O'Neal. These men and a few more of her crew survived, but most were drowned at sea. They were the first white men ever to set foot on Kinnakeet, N. C.

The Big Chief Indian was named Kinnakeet and his tribe was called "Kinnakeet" in his honor. He showed great hospitality, kindness, and concern for the unfortunate ones and took them to his wigwams and gave them food. The Kinnakeet Indian village was situated in the vicinity of the site on which the present Cape Hatteras Hotel is now located. This was a small tribe of Indians who had settled on and named their village Kinnakeet. They had found this place abundantly rich with fish, oysters, clams, ducks, geese, brant and every variety of wild birds. It was a food basket to satisfy the appetite of any prince. They also had their farms of corn and potatoes and vegetables.

The stranded sailors quickly adapted themselves and pleasantly made it their home and helped the Indians to hoe their fields, catch fish, trap ducks, and gladly follow the Indian in his way of life. They became members of the tribe and went through all the preliminary performances to become honorary members. They used their superior knowledge of technology and suavity and shortly became the bosses of the tribe. They used the Indians to help them to salvage the remains of their ship and used the timber to build homes. They also salvaged the tools, crockery, knives and forks and all the utensils that they could find for their home use. They intermarried and

10

ENGLISH GALLEON

This is a picture of an English galleon of the fourteenth, fifteenth, and sixteenth centuries.

This is a combination, warship and trader, which brought the English settlers to Roanoke Island, fought and captured

took unto themselves the young Indian lasses for their brides and raised children. Caleb Williams gave his wife an English name—he named her Sarah; David O'Neal called his wife "Morning Dew," and Elijah Scarborough named his wife "Olive."

Many other ships were stranded on the Kinnakeet beaches and their survivors were made members of the tribe and intermarried and through amalgamation the Indian disappeared and left no ethnic strain of his race. Sometimes you meet a woman with long straight black hair and high cheek bones; you wonder if that is an ethnic strain.

The legends of ancient Kinnakeet tradition says that a great friendship developed between the Kinnakeet and Croatan Indians and that they met in gala festive performances and that the Kinnakeet-stranded sailors became enamored of the Croatan women because of their similarity to the white race and that on several occasions they would marry in the Croatan tribe and bring their wives to Kinnakeet.

Spanish galleons, carrying gold and silver from Central and South America to Spain.

John White used the galleon type of ship on his fourth and fifth voyage to Virginia. On his fourth voyage to Roanoke Island which was then a part of Virginia, John White used two galleons, the *Admirall* and the *Lion* and "one flie boate."

On John White's fifth voyage he used three galleons, the *Hopewell, John Evangelist* and *Little John*.

This picture portrays the *John Evangelist,* that was caught in a hurricane east of Roanoke Island and east southeast of Kendricks Mount and was wrecked on the Kinnakeet Beach, and the survivors of her crew amalgamated with and became a part of the Kinnakeet Indian tribe.

This is traditional history of unquestioned veracity.

12

THE KINNAKEETER—THE INDIAN WOMAN HE MARRIED

The characteristics of the Indian man and woman that the shipwrecked sailors became a part of were nobleness, frugality and chastity. The man was industrious, a boatman, hunter and fisherman, truthful and honest. The woman had reached a high state of morality and prided herself on her chastity and love for her husband. She was to her husband a good, efficient and capable wife and mother, the kind that King Lemuel's mother taught him to seek. Her husband had no thought of guile and trusted her; she was obedient all the days of her life; she was frugal and helped him feed her children and cared for her household. She traded in the spiritual market of heaven. She bought her food of love, grace and kindness from the tables of heaven. She gave the food of love from the tree of life to her children and husband and a portion of love and joy to her neighbors. She perceives that her food, and her concern for her family does not fade in the darkness of night. She extends her hand to the poor and pleasantly she helps the needy. Her clothing is spiritual silk and purple and covers her person with a halo of glory woven and knitted with the needles of love from the looms of heaven. Strength and honor are her apparel and she will rejoice in time to come. She cares for her household and despises idleness. Her children love her and her husband gives her praise. She loves constancy and it cheers her neighbors like the gentle dew from heaven. She is one of the few great women of the world.

What a heritage the Kinnakeeter has in his ancient mother!

This is a John White drawing of an Algonquian town located at Kinnakinick, later known as Kinnakeet.

THE ALGONQUIANS

The Algonquians constructed towns on the same pattern throughout eastern North Carolina and eastern Virginia. They consisted of clusters of houses stockaded with poles set close together. The houses were designed in a rectangular shape. The Indians used vines and ropes tied at the top of wall poles to hold the roof and house sides together. The roof was made of bark. In the center of the floor was a fire pit used for cooking purposes. This house was usually called a wigwam.

Kinnakeet was an ideal, magnificent location for the Indian town to be erected. Food of every variety was in superabundance. Plants and animals were depended upon as the chief source of food. Fruits of various kinds, apples, peaches, pears and plums were plentiful. The Indians gathered berries, persimmons, nuts, roots and grapes, vegetables such as squash, beans, peas and corn. Corn was the chief crop of the farm. Food animals consisted of deer, squirrel, rabbit, muskrat, raccoon, opossum, fox and bear.

The ocean, sound, streams, ponds and estuary appendages were teeming with the greatest variety of edible fishes, clams, mussels and oysters in abundant profusion and with a delicious flavor. Birds of the air, willet, curlew, yellowlegs, snipe, sea chickens, herons, egrets, marsh hens, rail, scoggins, geese, brant, red head, black duck, teal, canvasback, mallard and every variety of ducks from the northern provinces of Canada, filled the sounds and marshes in darkening clouds. The Algonquians were supplied with the most luscious breadbasket of the American Continent.

INDIAN CANOE

This is a picture of Algonquin Indians building a boat at Kinnakeet with fire and stone axes. It is a reproduction from an engraving of John White's watercolor.

They used a tall tree sufficient in diameter to make a boat that was seaworthy and capable of navigating the waters adjacent to Kinnakeet. After stripping the bark off the tree with sharp shells a fire was made all along the trunk of the tree; then they had the tedious job as the boat burned to keep the burned wood off. This burning and scraping went on for a long time.

INDIANS FISHING

This is a picture of the Algonquin Indians fishing in the ancient estuaries and shallow rivers along the Kinnakeet Sound shore line. Fish are plentiful and can be caught with spear, weir and dip nets. Fishing was remunerative the year around and afforded them a continuous abundant supply of food summer and winter. The abundant supply of fish, clams, oysters, ducks, geese and shore birds throughout Hatteras Island was the main reason that so many Indians made it their permanent home and their way of livelihood is still prevalent to this day. They lived on the luscious joy of sport.

They were proud and adorned their necks with gorgeous strings of beads of pearls of exquisite beauty.

Their tools were made of bone, canes, wood and shell.

The Algonquians were a devout religious people. They worshipped the sun, wind, water, fire, lightning, thunder and most other forces in nature.

Each season of the year they had important ceremonies to celebrate. The most impoitant was the corn gathering festival. The mainland Indian would assemble at the Kinnakeet Indians' wigwam and dance, drink, eat and sing for weeks in joyous celebration. The cassina, or youpon, leaves would be brewed and they would drink excessively to a drunken stupor. They played their music on flutes made of reeds and covered with copper.

These Algonquians were the earliest Indians to come in contact with the English settlers of Roanoke Island under the direction of Sir Walter Raleigh. They were the first to war with and the first to trade with the colonists under John White.

They contracted the white man's diseases, such as small-pox, measles and venereal diseases, which decimated their numbers and brought them near to their extinction. The Algonquian Indians of Kinnakeet were not decimated by disease or war. They just faded away by amalgamation and intermarriage with shipwrecked English sailors who were stranded in increasing numbers on the Kinnakeet beach.

Their ancient moral behavior and culture just melted and died in the more advanced culture of their English conquerors and masters and from this union or reconciliation of two adverse cultures evolved the most unique race of people of the New World called the Kinnakeeter.

COLONIZATION

First Settlers

Kinnakeet was peopled and settled under the mysterious guidance of the Divine Majesty of God working with and through storms and situational environment to colonize the right type of people fitted for the rigors of a lonely life born of desperation and fortitude. Sailing ships, plying the coastal waters from Central America and South America, Florida, Charleston, South Carolina, and Wilmington, North Carolina, enroute to Boston, Philadelphia, Baltimore and Norfolk, Virginia, or from New England, New York, Philadelphia, Baltimore and Norfolk enroute to Wilmington, North Carolina, Charleston, South Carolina, ports in Florida and the West Indies, encountered storms of hurricane force off the North Carolina coast. They were driven on the beaches and quickly disintegrated and went to pieces in the terrific pounding of the awesome power of angry waves. The seamen that luckily made the shore alive quickly acclimated themselves to their environment, made friends with the Indians. Aware that they were out of contact with the outside world, they instantly loved their new home with a zealous jealousy. Each new storm their numbers were augmented by other shipwrecked sailors. Their population grew fast; they came in increasing numbers. The Austins, Barnetts, Ballances, Burrus, Dixons, Farrows, Grays, Midgetts, Millers, Morgans, O'Neals, Prices, Peeles, Quidleys, Scarboroughs, Williamses and a host of others, including a few of Jewish origin.

Their Way of a New Life

Acclimating themselves to a new life amid an Indian culture, they quickly adjusted themselves to the way of the red man, friendly with the Indians, enjoying their hospitality. They suavely applied the golden rule to their dealings with their new found friends, "Do unto others that you would have them to do unto you." In perfect freedom they lived happily in their new home. Their mode of travel was by foot or Indian canoe. They hollowed cedar logs and built beautiful canoes of curvaceous design, also they built two-masted schooners. They learned to sweat hot stones and brew cassina or youpon tree leaves for their drink. This they learned from the Indians. During the feast of the corn festival the Indians drank this tea to stupid drunkenness. Of salt, a needed commodity, they had none. They made wooden vats and placed them near the oceanside, filled them with sea water and then gathered the salt after the water evaporated. They would kill their cattle, pigs, and salt their beef and pork, catch fish by spear and net, and salt their fish. Having no matches, they got fire by rubbing sticks together until they blazed or went to their neighbor for hot coals to start their fires. They built homes from logs, used wooden fireplaces and wooden windows. Because of no screening, they suffered terribly from mosquitoes and flies. During the summer months, they salted their fish and carried them to the mainland and traded them for corn and potatoes, returned home and stored the produce in their attics, and then settled down for a long winter's night of fun. They whooped it up under the music of the fiddler's bow. Old Virginia Reel was the popular number.

Chap Lincoln was an accomplished fiddler and usually was the master of ceremonies.

INDUSTRY

Timber

In 1776 the thirteen states declared themselves free and independent from English rule and tyranny, and under the providence of God set up a new nation among the nations of the earth. North Carolina shortly became one of the dominant prosperous states of the original colonies.

In this ancient day Kinnakeet quickly expanded and became the most aristocratic, populous and wealthiest village on the Outer Banks of North Carolina.

The wealth was controled by an English squire named Pharaoh Farrow who had at his command hundreds of slaves and was the largest real estate owner on the Outer Banks. His land was covered by a dense forest of giant oaks, a magnificent hard wood, suitable for framing the hulls of the Yankee Clipper fleet of the sailing ships. By use of slave labor he cut down these beautiful spreading trees and trimmed the branches and took the limbs that were suitable for framing to muddy glades and immersed them in the muddy waters for preservation, and sold this oak timber to the shipbuilders of New England. Fleets of sail-ship freighters came down the coast and entered Kenna Cut Inlet and moored at the Great Island just at the north edge of Kinnakeet village and loaded this timber. This was a lucrative industry, but did not add any monetary economic life to the village because all labor was performed by slaves.

The cash proceeds went into the money bags or trunks of

Pharaoh Farrow. He grew immensely rich in gold, perhaps the wealthiest man that ever lived in Eastern North Carolina. You have heard it said "you can't take it with you," so he left his fortune at Kinnakeet.

Many tales and legends exist to this day as to how he disposed of his fortune. After he had cut down all the oaks and denuded the land, he had no further need for slaves. He took them to the slave markets and auctioned them to the highest bidder. For this vast number of slaves he reaped a fabulous fortune. Keeping a few slaves for his personal use, the legend is when he was old and getting ready to depart from this earthly scene and return to his Maker, being on his deathbed, he called his faithful slaves and bade them to build a brick cistern underground and bury his gold-laden trunks, so heavy that two of his neighbors, on a visit to bid him farewell, were asked to try and lift an end of one of his trunks, and it was so heavy they failed in the attempt. The whereabouts of this burial site has been a question much discussed by the village folk. Many places and theories as to the burial place has been advanced.

There is no doubt but that it was north of Thomas Gray's home, placing it on the Henderson Scarborough tract of land in the vicinity of the present homes of Erving Gray, Collins Gray or Basil Hopper.

My uncle Ben Scarborough and George Moran visited a seer or fortune teller and she told them that near a certain oak stump was buried treasure in a trunk. They dug and found a brick cistern. Someone was passing and they covered the hole expecting at some more opportune day they would return and finish the job. That new day never came.

The slaves that moved to Hyde County after Mr. Farrow died, coming in contact with some Kinnakeeters that were in Englehard on business, told them the burial site of his trunks. Now the trunks in silent repose are sleeping in the voiceless dust of the earth of Kinnakeet, awaiting for someone digging the foundation for a new home to unearth the largest buried fortune of this century.

Fishing

Since time immemorial man has gone down to the sea fishing. Fishing has been an economic income and source of food for all nations bordering the oceans, seas and rivers. When the first settlers made Kinnakeet their home, it was their chief source of food and medium of exchange. With the people on the mainland, they engaged in a system of barter trade —salt fish for corn and sweet potatoes. They put their entire time during the summer months salting mullet and spats. The most industrious men of the village purchased their salt fish for about four or five dollars per barrel, paid the people cash for the fish and in October they carried the fish to the mainland and exchanged fish for corn and potatoes and other vegetables and sold the corn and potatoes to the poorer natives for a small profit. Watson Gray and Harris Miller built fish and ice houses on stilts or pilings about a thousand feet out from the shore line in the Pamlico Sound and at intervals brought ice from Elizabeth City and Washington, N. C., and purchased fresh fish. They made weekly trips to Elizabeth City and Washington, N. C., and sold them to retail fish dealers and county fish hucksters. The schooner boat operating to Elizabeth City was the *H. P. Brown*. The boat operating to Washington, N. C., was the *Carrie Bell*.

Oystering

Kinnakeeters were excellent boat builders, and had built a trim fleet of two-masted schooners, fifty or more for the winter oyster trade. They were masters of the Pamlico, Core and Bogue Sound oyster beds. They tonged and dredged oysters from Roanoke Island to the southern oyster rocks of Carteret County. They sold their oysters wholesale in Elizabeth City and Washington, N. C., and kept the dealers in abundant supply for twenty-five cents per bushel. The owners of smaller boats carried their oysters to Columbia, Hertford, Edenton,

Elizabeth City, Great Bridge and a host of other small towns and villages and retailed their catch for fifty cents per bushel in the shell or sold by measure at fifty cents per pint, and also engaged in barter trade with the farmers—oysters for corn.

Livestock Raising

Kinnakeet was a free range. Animals roamed the village and marshes at will. There was no lone prairie; every man knew his own animals, though they roamed and mingled together. Every stock owner had his own private mark and branding iron. At intervals, they penned their stock in what they called cow pounds, and each man marked and branded his calves, colts and lambs. Stock buyers were constantly passing through the village purchasing cattle, horses and sheep. They loaded them on pontoons or waded them out in the sound to the boat and hoisted them on board. This boat was to carry them to Elizabeth City, North Carolina, Washington, N. C., or Norfolk, Virginia. It was an exciting time for the small boys to watch them penning and loading the animals on board the boats. The animals were so numerous they finally denuded the land of grass and tender vegetation and large numbers died from starvation. Many of them in early Spring mired in muddy marshes and muddy glades trying to reach a free pasture.

Luscious feeding ranges became blowing sand, and the Texas fever tick depleted their ranks. The State enacted a no-free-range law and a compulsory dipping law to try to eradicate the Texas fever tick. This law caused much confusion and dissatisfaction. People that did not have time to dip their stock failed to show up on dipping days and were eager to sell their stock at any price offered them.

Frank Miller owned a herd of thirty beef steers, best grades of milk cows and beautiful heifers and offered to sell the entire herd for sixty dollars.

At that time I was operating two large trucks to Norfolk,

Virginia, and carried out loads of poor cows, barely alive, reeling as they walked; also loads of sheep, just a bunch of shaggy wool and skin stretched over a slender bone. Thanks to Edgar Miller and Ernest Quidley, the range riders rounded up the herds, supervised the chemical vats and saw that all stock was dipped before leaving Kinnakeet.

Wool

Hundreds of sheep roamed this free range. Two or three men owned all the sheep. There were two large sheep pens and during the early days the word was passed "sheep penning today" and everybody left their work and helped the sheep owners corral their sheep. This was the day to mark the lambs and shear the sheep. The wool was shipped to wool markets in Elizabeth City, or Norfolk, Virginia. The sheep owners reaped a handsome profit from the sale of their wool. Many families owned no sheep and had no wool. During the night, sheep roamed and nipped the tender leaves from low bushes and shrubbery, and would leave a large quantity of wool entangled in the shrubbery. In the early morning, the families that had no sheep would send their children through the woods picking wool from the bushes that the sheep had left during the night.

Some older women owned old-fashioned spinning wheels. They would card and spin this wool into yarn thread on a fifty per cent basis. The people prided themselves as fancy expert knitters of socks, gloves, sweaters, and knitted woolen goods for their family for the coming winter.

Baling Seaweed

P. W. Midgett, a Kinnakeeter, and a sailboat captain on the Schooner *Thelma G.* operating from Washington, North Carolina, to Norfolk, Virginia, on one of his trips to the loading piers in Norfolk, saw a shipment of baled seaweed, proper

25

name—eel grass, consigned to C. T. Winchester, Baltimore, Maryland. On his next trip enroute to Norfolk he stopped over at Kinnakeet for the night and told my father what he had seen. At that time, Kinnakeet was the potential seaweed capital of the world.

My father communicated with Mr. Winchester by letter and he offered to purchase all the seaweed that Father could bale. Mr. Winchester was a seaweed broker and had a large outlet for the weed which was used by furniture manufacturers. After the furniture had been sandpapered, the seaweed was used to put a finishing gloss to the furniture, and for mattress filling which was superior to cotton. Mr. Winchester sent my father a wooden baler, and we began to spread and dry the weed for baling.

My father, my brother Evin, and myself pooled our resources and sent Evin to Carteret County to purchase a boat to freight the weed to the railway freight station in Elizabeth City, for transshipment to Baltimore, Md. Others shortly started bailing the weed. F. L. Scarborough and his boys with helpers, D. F. Meekins and C. T. Godwin purchased a regular horse-driven baler like they used to bale hay with. A baling crew established a large seaweed drying business at Little Kinnakeet. The industry boomed for several years and was very lucrative.

Some mysterious phenomenon, a natural minute animalcule, attacked the weed at its roots and killed it. This eel grass was the natural food for brant, geese and several species of ducks, but more particularly for brant. When they returned from their breeding grounds the next season, the major part of their food was gone. They died by the thousands and came near extinction. This deadly minute organism attacked the eel grass all the way from Canada to South America, but did not affect the West Coast of the United States.

There was a ready market for all the weed that we could bale, in New York, Chicago, Baltimore, Norfolk and High Point, and all mattress and furniture manufacturers in the State of North Carolina. That small bug killed our business one day.

Wildfowl Hunting

During the month of March, the inherent urge to mate and propagate their kind makes millions of brant, geese, and ducks of all varieties unceasingly restless. They begin to hobnob in a hoity-toity chattering way and assemble their clans together and at the proper moment the leader spreads his wings and soars in the skies, circles his awaiting companions and one by one they ascend in flight, forming a perfect *v* formation. A few more circles help them get their instinctive compass bearings and off to the Arctic nesting and laying grounds, in a few days of flight to their summer home. It is cool, some snow still bedecking the land with Arctic beauty. God has covered the cranberry bogs with a garment of spotless white, snow preserving the berries, their food awaiting them.

They are now home enjoying a summer vacation. They build their nest, lay their eggs, hatch their young. In late October their summer vacation ended, the sting of wintry blasts sweeps the Arctic and covers their feeding grounds of cranberries with a snowy carpet. Another hobnob chattering, another gathering, their leader running fast unfurls his wings and zooms in the air. Others follow in quick succession. They form their natural *v* formation. Their numbers increased with young, they make their circle gathering their brood, get their bearings and with exact precision start on their long journey for Kinnakeet, North Carolina. They arrive on schedule, cross this small ribbon of land lying thirty miles out in the Atlantic go direct to their feeding grounds on the reefs on the west side of Kinnakeet in the Pamlico Sound. The geese herald a salute to the village folk in the midnight with their familiar honk.

Heartless man gets his gun ready for a winter of torture and inhumane slaughter, making it a Winter of chaos and cold night for God's birds that he has painted so beautifully, the hunter has all his paraphernalia ready in advance for the ensuing winter of massacre.

Night and day they come in increasing numbers,

thousands of geese, brant, redhead, canvasback, black duck, teal, widgeon and all manner of the feathered tribe in exquisite beauty and innocence. They soon learn the depths of man's fall from grace. His battery with its deck is painted, his decoys in shape. His battery is a box, six to eight feet long, about three foot wide, the deck is a large floor with a hole in the center of it. In this hole they place the battery; it is used as a breakwater to keep the water out of the battery. This is a movable portable outfit and can be carried to any place along the reef that is best suitable for the day's kill.

The hunter has also an unmovable cement box buried in the shallow water fitted with a canvas neck to keep out the water. He also has a blind built on stilts or piling. This is a wooden box camouflaged with rushes and small shrubbery. Decoys made of wood and painted in exact similitude of geese and ducks are scattered around his battery, cement box or blind. The reef is now alive with wild ducks of every variety and the skies are darkened with vast flocks of ducks and the unfair game of human deception decoying the innocent unsuspecting birds to their death begins.

The marketing of slaughtered game was quite an economic asset to the Kinnakeeter. With no bag limit, hunters could kill indiscriminately by the hundreds, preferring redhead, and canvasback which brought a handsome price on the big city markets, such as New York, Philadelphia, and Baltimore. They sold in pairs, bringing four to six dollars per pair. After the Federal Government put bag limits on a day's kill and heavy penalities on the sale of wild fowl, hunters catered to the transient sportsman, which became profitable for a few years. This catering is near extinction. Hunting wild fowl now is a pleasure only to the illegal poacher, who always stands in fear of a game warden.

WILDFOWL
These are pictures of Canadian geese and a blue goose and mallards. These birds are highly prized for food birds and in the past years were slaughtered by the thousands.

Coast Guard

The most important and far-reaching monetary contribution to the economic life of Kinnakeet was the building of Coast Guard land-based stations at Big Kinnakeet and the Outer Banks. The Kinnakeeters, being seafaring men, immediately enlisted in all the stations, and filled all vacancies as quickly as they could. This gave them steady employment and monthly pay, something they were not used to. Self-employment had always been their way of life. This steady employment revolutionized their basic way of a monetary life. It raised their standard of living, fed their family, built their homes, and gave their children a better life.

They followed the Coast Guard beyond the boundaries of the Outer Banks. Their young men enlisted in land-based stations on the New York, New Jersey, Virginia, Texas and Florida coasts, and on seagoing cutters and other installations throughout the United States. Kinnakeet has contributed more men to the Coast Guard service than any village of comparable size in the United States. Enlistment in the Coast Guard service is a continuous way of life for the Kinnakeeter. Making it a career, seeking the benefits of retirement, they serve from twenty to thirty years to achieve this goal. Throughout the world wherever you find Coast Guard cutters or land-based stations, you will find the Kinnakeeter. Wherever the Coast Guard is employed in peace, hazardous rescue work, or in the horrors of war, the Kinnakeeter is there playing a heroic part.

WAY OF LIFE

Windmill

The windmill was brought to Kinnakeet by Pharaoh Farrow, the English squire, to grind corn into meal to feed his slaves who worked in his lumber industry from the West Indies. On small peninsulas of land jutting out into the Pamlico Sound he erected his mills. These mills were situated on these peninsulas because there was no vegetation to impede the force of wind which was used as power to operate the mill. There were two of these mills which were purchased from Pharaoh Farrow by the Miller family and Scarborough family. The mills were a huge structure on a metal axis or swivel, so that the mill could be turned in any direction desired. They had two large millstones, an upper one and another which was used to grind the corn into fine meal. These mills finally became the property of Bateman Miller and F. L. Scarborough.

When the wind would blow from the southwest a brisk breeze, they would spread their sails and start the mill in operation. The village folk would bring their corn and the mill owner would grind it into meal for a small toll of the meal for which they had a special place. That was the way they got their meal.

One day at the Miller mill a peculiar situation occurred. Mr. Miller went out on the mill wings to spread his sails. When he had finished spreading the sails, his son Jones, a mentally retarded youth, released the levers prematurely and Mr. Miller was the recipient of an unwanted free ride into space.

AVON WINDMILL

MILLSTONE

This photograph is a picture of one of the two millstones used in the Bateman Miller Windmill at Kinnakeet, N.C. The other stone is broken and not fit for use as an illustration. Both stones are of exact size and were used to grind corn, and used as an upper and nether stone for fine grinding.

RECREATION

Sugar Boiling

The most gleeful game was sugar boiling, known as candy pulling. The young men purchased sugar, and, with the girls, assembled in their neighbors' home and put large pans on the stove over a slow fire. While the sugar was boiling for pulling into candy, they would engage in singing love songs. Blivens Scarborough and Bill Jim Gray were the star attractions. They were accomplished crooner singers and brought tears to many lovers' hearts. The young people played various games for entertainment. The most exciting game was a kissing spree performed by the youngest girl. Everyone was quiet, everyone looking, waiting for something to happen. The beautiful one flitted across the floor, placed her back to the wall and in a loving girlish coquettish voice said:

"Here I stand under the latch, twenty kisses make me a match; more kisses more fun, come and kiss me everyone."

A mad scramble ensues to be the first one to get the prize kiss. That night will be remembered by the kissed one.

The sugar partially cooled is now ready for pulling into candy. The boy and girl face each other, the boy extends his right hand toward the girl, the girl extends her right hand toward the boy. Both clasp the sugar at the same time, pull back toward themselves, then the boy extends his left hand toward the girl and the girl extends her left hand toward the boy and pull back toward themselves. This operation continues until the sugar turns white and hardens. Candy of the finest kind is now made and can be weaved into any shape or design that suits their taste.

Sail Skiff Racing

In the latter part of the 18th Century, the Kinnakeeters were master boatbuilders. They built fleets of two-masted schooners, sturdy and beautifully designed. They developed a unique sail skiff, 18 to 30 feet in length. They used a portable mast with mainsail, and jib attached to spread the mainsail. They used a wooden sprit, also; in the ce..ter of the skiff, they attached a center board to diminish leeway while in operation. A portable rudder for steering was used. For ballast, there were canvas bags filled with sand which they shifted from gunwale to gunwale while in operation; also, at times a ballast board with one end tucked under the gunwale and extending across the midsection of the skiff and protruding over the other gunwale of the reverse side about four or five feet. A man would crawl out to the end of the board to be used as ballast. This was the most efficient ballast they could use.

Each man being a fisherman and fishing alone owned his own skiff. Probably fifty to seventy-five skiffs were at all times anchored on the Pamlico side of the village. The fishermen were always arguing who had the fastest skiff and to prove who had the fastest skiff, they would arrange a race on Saturday, if the wind was blowing a very strong gale to the Southwest. It would be an eight-mile race from the shore line to the Inner Buoy at the Cape Channel and back to land. Ten to twenty skiffs would participate and one or two canoes would be in the race. Some of the skiffs would be dead-rise, chime or chimp-bottomed, some flat-bottomed. Every participating skiff ready, all sails set and manned, awaiting the word to go; the signal given, the big race is on. Who will be

36

the winner? That depends on who will be the helmsman, and the set of his sail. It's a tough watery race. Mitchell Gray usually captained his father's canoe. He was a master of the art of skiff sailing. Generally he was the winner. Three or four hundred village people crowded the shore line, lots of arguments going on. Some would say, "Gray is ahead." Someone else would holler out, "Miller is gaining on Gray." This talk seesawed back and forth, all eyes straining to see the first skiff to reach the buoy and shift his course back shoreward.

The mainsail is now spread out on a main boom, the jib spread out on the opposite side by the jib boom. Steadily the wind increases, the skiff actually begins to fly, just the stern end of the skiff touching water deep enough to steer the skiff. A wonderfully entrancing sight to behold, every skiff in perfect orderly formation. Fleeting like soaring birds they reach the shore line in a majesty that reflects the honor of the racing participants. The race is over and Gray is the winner.

Horse Racing

Most of the young Kinnakeeters enlisted in the U. S. Coast Guard, on land-based stations at Big Kinnakeet, Little Kinnakeet, Cape Hatteras, and Clarks. During the summer months they did not stay at the stations, so they had lots of leisure time to engage in some kind of sports. They purchased the most beautiful, fleetest horses that they could find and during the summer months they became avid horse-racing fiends. The most elaborate, beautiful natural race track in the world was on the Kinnakeet flats. They participated in races every Saturday. The village folk attended, cheering the winner.

Jesse Thomas Gray, a dashing, brilliant young sport, went to the mainland and purchased a thoroughbred race horse, spirited, and of noble appearance, roan-colored, a specimen of beauty. When racing, he was a cloud of moving sand. Mr. Gray won all races; no bets, no gambling, just a joyful happy entertainment for the leisurely Kinnakeeter who became a horse-racing fan.

Cat

Kinnakeeters have enjoyed more leisure time than most any people in the world. They have always employed this leisure time to healthful body building and mental development. One of the oldest games was a game called Cat. This game in similarity is almost a duplicate of baseball; the same number of bases, a home plate, pitcher, catcher, infielders and outfielders. The ball they used was made of wool, spun into wool thread with a rag core in order to put the batter out after he had hit the ball. The fielder getting the ball must hit the batter by throwing the ball at him. Some batters were fast runners and high jumpers and adept at eluding the ball. One old man by the name of Banister Gray was never known to be hit by the ball; he always made his base. It was a strenuous game and usually played on Sunday afternoon by the adult people. Exciting and full of entertainment, the Kinnakeeters turned out enmasse and cheered their favorite team.

Checkers

Checkers is a game of brain, mind, and patience, anticipating the move of your opponent. This game was a home game and all members of the family were good players. The best players gathered at the neighborhood store at night. Most everyone had a favorite move and I usually noticed that the man that used the V-formation move usually won if he could see far enough to pursue it through. This game was the favorite winter game.

Croquet

Croquet was a dignified princely game and some players knew just how hard to hit the ball so it would go through the wickets and stop at the desired place. It was a game that appealed to the older men and gave them a chance to use their mind in a precise effort to embellish their mentality.

Baseball

The game of Cat was fast dying and near extinction at Kinnakeet, and baseball was being organized by a schoolteacher, C. T. Godwin, and he was thrilling the young boys of his school about the game and organized a team. Their parents, sensing the quality of the game, became enthused to the extent that they stopped all work and attended all of the games and became expert analysts of baseball rules and regulations. They knew more about the rules than they did their Bible. Any small error started fierce arguments that waxed strong throughout the game. The boys mastered the game in quick order and soon became champions and won the major part of the games with Hatteras, Stumpy Point, and Manteo.

Baxter Gray was the pitcher and he had perfect control of the ball. He threw a very fast ball with a beautiful curve. He struck out most everyone who came to bat, with a ball that passed just a fraction below the shoulder of the batter. Dick Scarborough was the argumentative catcher and so fast he caught most all fly foul balls. Ellis Gray was the first baseman and never missed a ball thrown to him. Calvin Meekins was shortstop and used his body as a wall against a line drive. The fielders never missed a fly ball. The Kinnakeeter believed that their team could easily have beaten the Yankees or the Boston Braves.

Pirates' Jamboree

In 1955, the Outer Banks put on an interesting entertainment of horse racing, buggy racing, a giant free fish fry, and many other exhibitions of interest to the public called the Pirates' Jamboree. It was highlighted by the pirates' beard. The Kinnakeeter was there sporting his well kept Peter Stuyvesant beard, and prominent upturned Russian Finn moustache.

CAPE HATTERAS LIGHTHOUSE

This is a photograph of the Cape Hatteras Lighthouse erected in 1870, and a large fish fry, a festive occasion of splendid entertainment for the hungry after a day of beach-buggy racing and horse racing by ponies and riders from Ocracoke, North Carolina. This photograph was taken by Aycock Brown, the adept, proficient and efficient chief of the Dare County Tourist Bureau, who by his suave advertising to the tourist of the world has put Dare County on the map of the world and brought millions of tourists and visitors to the county, and enhanced the monetary value of Dare County to a transcendent height of gold and bright polished silver. The Kinnakeeter is proud of Aycock, an affable and kindly personality to all that come in contact with him.

This photograph is featuring the first Outer Banks Pirate Jamboree, 1955.

41

FESTIVITIES

Corn Festival

The first festive merrymaking that the early Kinnakeeter participated in was in conjunction with the Indians in their corn festival celebrating the harvest of corn. The Indians came to the Outer Banks and spent about two weeks of gala merrymaking, dancing and drinking to stupid drunkenness on brewed cassina leaves.

Christmas

The celebration of Christmas is ancient and has been from time immemorial. The most celebrated gala, festive, spiritual-connected merrymaking performance of all time. The Kinnakeeter started about two months before Christmas Day to start his festivities. The merchants stocked their stores with quantities of fireworks including Roman candles, firecrackers, rockets, Dewey bombs; brandy and apple cider as well. Day and night the air was filled with the noise of firecrackers, Roman candles and Dewey bombs. Rockets lighted the night skies with fantastic, beautiful colors.

The young boys began to do what they called "dressing up," by taking a black stocking, cutting holes for eyes and mouth and circling the eyes and mouth with white embroidery, making and sèwing on the stocking long red noses out of red flannel, then stretching the stocking over their heads. Some boys would burn cork wood and paint their faces black, red circle their mouth and eyes. Each night they would go on a gala warpath visiting their neighbors, eating their fresh cooked pies, playing the harmonica and dancing on their porches, having themselves a good time.

The old men would make ready for the big day, Christmas itself. They took a big pole, attached a bleached cow's head, and barrel hoops for a body and ribs, and covered it with dry cow skins. Two men, one in the front and one in the tail end, would get beneath it perfectly hidden. Ready to start on a village march at noon, John Quidley would beat the drum and Henry Scarborough would blow the fife. This really attracted the people. Starting at the church door, at the beating of the drum and blowing of the fife, people would pour out from their homes and fall in line. As they circled the village, all the people, children and barking dogs would shortly be in the march. For hours the celebration lasted. The old cow was the center of attraction.

Old men and old women were scared and would run for cover when the old cow went on a rampage, kicking and snorting. Children would cry and the dogs would bark and run in all directions. The day ended in joy and happiness. Hungry, they all ate a large supper, and then off to church for the large Christmas tree, lighted with candles, loaded with presents. Usually I would read the name of the person on the package, and ushers would go through the congregation and deliver the gifts. The church was packed with hundreds of people and everyone received a gift.

The most interesting part of Christmas for the children was Christmas Eve night. The small children went to bed early, lay in bed and whispered, waiting for Santa to come down the chimney from the far North with a heavy pack of toys and fill their stockings. In the early morning, while it was still dark, they would jump out of bed and run to their stockings. All would get nice presents. The boys preferred a five-cent pack of Chinese firecrackers, a pistol and fire caps. The girl always looked for her doll, a package of raisins, a box of candy and an orange. Christmas is now over; they wait gleefully for the approach of the next Christmas.

NATIVE COURTSHIP

Love, wooing your bride or husband, is the most fascinating experience of young lovers. It is the most entrancing impulse of inherent desire implanted in the soul of man by God. Adam was a violent lover. To him his bride was flesh of his flesh; to us Christ is the perfect example of courtship. Seeking His bride from all races of humanity, He is the big lover of all; He loves all His lovers and jilts none. Love, courtship and marriage is the apex of beauty, comfort, and joy to young lovers.

In the seclusion and isolation of Kinnakeet is the perfect Garden of Eden for wooing lovers. Miles of beautiful beaches at low tide are a paradise for horse-and-buggy rides made for two to lose their young hearts. Lonely trails and roads, such as the old Kinnakeet Buxton road and winding roads that connect Kinnakeet, Little Kinnakeet, Clarks, and Chicamacomico, riding these trails and roads by horse and buggy was an enticing adventure, especially when revival meetings were going on in these villages. A young man would chase his horse six miles in order to drive him four miles at night to carry his girl friend to the revival meeting. These young braves of Kinnakeet would go through rain, snow, and wintry blast to court their love.

All young people attended Sunday morning church services, then rushed home to a dinner of collard greens and salt pork, beans and pork, or chicken and dumplings, yearning for Sarah Hills. After a short fellowship meeting they would pair off in couples and make love under the shade of spreading

47

oaks, a place of hilly beauty for an evening courtship. Then a lazy walk to the oceanside, hand in hand, they made their way to the ocean. Beautiful beaches, and curlew, willet, and sea chickens playing, seagulls flying around them almost talking and watching them with peering eyes, seeming to be conscious of their loving intentions. The moon just beginning to rise over the eastern horizon was throwing her beams of shimmering moonlight on the peaceful water and in this aura of moonlight beauty a Sunday in this paradise of courtship had reached its finale.

Hand in hand they return to the village and go to their neighbor's home for a gala, festive, old-fashioned love singspiration, finishing with the crooning voices of Blivens Scarborough and the chief of love song crooner, William Gray, who was lovingly called Bill Jim.

Now sleepy they go to bed, and have beautiful dreams of courtship, love and marriage. Upon awakening they examine themselves, and it is all a vast dream.

EDUCATION

Village School Life

Educating their children so they could compete with a contemporary world was of paramount importance. The state provided no schoolhouses or teachers. They built a small community school and public-spirited men and women volunteered to act as teachers. Their only books were a Webster blue-back speller and some form of a church catechism. This system went on for many decades. Among these teachers were Henderson Scarborough and my grandmother, Christine Williams. They taught the two aspects of life—spiritual and moral ethics.

After many years the school system improved and the state sent teachers to the village, and they taught in abandoned homes and storehouses. Later, the village was divided into two school districts, one on Cat Ridge and one on Dog Ridge. Finally the state decided to build a nice modest school building. Friction developed among the people as to where the building should be located. The battle seesawed between the Cat Ridgers and Dog Ridgers sparring to have the building in their district. Finally a vote for consolidation was taken, and the consolidationists won and the building was placed in the center of the village. A large commodious, imposing building was erected to take care of the needs of the people for many years.

After a few years of enjoying a great success, the State Board of Education deemed it wise to consolidate all the schools on Hatteras Island into one modern high school. A battle royal of immense proportation developed between the Hatteras and Kinnakeet townships sparring for the location of the school building. After two or three years of bitterness, investigations, public meetings between the contestants the fight was ended and the State finally located this grand educational edifice at Buxton, North Carolina, on Cape Hatteras. All traces of bitterness are now healed and the school is marching smoothly and successfully to a pleasant future. This is the culmination of two hundred years of school preparation by the first citizen of Kinnakeet, North Carolina. This is a glorious finale to the image of education and knowledge.

RELIGIOUS LIFE

The Indians

The Kinnakeet Indian was the first original Kinnakeeter, a small tribe that was originally known as the Kinniki-nick tribe, a segment of the Algonquian tribe and who spoke the Algonquian language. The tribe was by nature a very religious tribe of people in quest of the identity of the one and only true God. The Kinnakeet Indian had religion of a nature that was not true but was satisfactorily accepted by them, a religion by tradition handed down to them by their fathers. Their belief was there were many gods of different kinds and degrees of excellence, but only one great God, who was great and who had always inhabited the Universe; that he made other gods first to be the means and instruments used in the creation, such as suns, moon and stars as petty gods. They say that the waters were made first, and that out of the waters all creation visible and invisible were created. They believe that woman was made first and by the working of one of the lesser gods conceived and brought forth children.

They think that all gods are of human shape and they represent them by images in the form of man; they place them in a house or temple, where they worship, sing and pray and make offerings unto them.

They believe that the soul is immortal and after the soul is departed from the body, if it has performed good works it will

51

be carried to heaven the home of the Great God, there to enjoy eternal happiness. Or if their works performed have been evil, the soul will be taken to a great pit or hole toward the farthest part of the world, toward the setting sun; this place they call Popogusso. To confirm this opinion as a place for sinful departed spirits, they relate a weird story of a man being dead and buried. The earth of his grave was seen to vividly move. He was unearthed and taken up again and he declared that his soul was near entering Popogusso and one of the gods saved him and gave him a permit to return to earth and warn his friends what they should do to avoid this terrible place.

They relate a similar story of another man being dead, buried and taken up again. His body had lain in the grave, yet his soul was alive and had traveled far on a long broadway. On each side of the broadway grew beautiful delicate trees, bearing rare and wonderful fruits like he had never seen before. He was unable to express their beauty and at the end of the broadway he came to a beautiful house or temple of one of the gods. Near the temple he met his father who had departed this life many years before. His father told him to go back to earth again and tell his friends what good works they must perform in order to enjoy the pleasures of abode of departed spirits. When he had delivered the message, he should come back again.

The Kinnakeeter, a new member of the Kinnakeet tribe of Indians, brought his Bible from his shipwrecked ship and taught the Indians the true religion of one God, and declared unto them the unsearchable riches of God, His love and saving grace. When the Indians understood the real God they clasped the Bible to their bosoms and, with penitent tears streaming down their bronzed faces, lavishly and unceasingly kissed the Bible of the Kinnakeeter.

When the King of the Kinnakeeters had a premonitory call from his God that the time of his departure had come to follow the setting sun to the land of Popogusso, he ordered his priest to brew a large cup of cassina from the leaves of the cassina tree and pass the cup around to his assembled mourn-

52

ers. No one was allowed to drink except those who have proven their valor in battle. When the King peacefully passed away into the land of Popogusso, his eternal resting place, they buried him with the dance of tearful mourning around his funeral bier. They buried in his grave the cup of cassina which to him will be the drink of the waters of life to his soul in its voyage to his beloved Popogusso. Around his grave they stuck many arrows to frighten away the evil spirits on his way to his Happy Hunting Ground. This feasting and weeping at a tribal funeral is an imposing finale to the Kinnakeeters' last King.

The Churches

Shipwrecked sailors, the first settlers of Kinnakeet, brought with them a heart of love abounding in the grace of God and constant fidelity of friendship and love for Jesus Christ. They kept the faith and strengthened their faith and belief. They raised their children in the nurture and admonition of the Lord. They had no church building for assembly worship. They went from neighbor's home to neighbor's home for singing, shouting, and praising the Lord. On Sunday they gathered at the school building for worship and taught their children to fellowship with each other. They taught them that God is a spirit, that God is love, that God is everywhere.

Their souls yearned for a church building. They wanted a place they could call God's temple, His holy house. Seemingly there was no chance for that. They were poverty-stricken, never saw much gold or silver. Wealth for them was salt beef, salt pork, and heartburn from sweet potatoes. The reward from their wealth malnutrition was a short life, therefore, a man that lived twenty-five years was considered a very old man.

The great Civil War had ended. Foreign troops occupied their homeland and poverty stalked every avenue of their life.

In 1880, God remembered their groans, their cry, and their petitions to Him, and answered their prayer for a church building at Kinnakeet. God wrought a miracle on their behalf.

He came down to Cape Channel and adjoining muddy sound bottoms and planted hundreds of thousands of bushels of oysters in the muddy bottoms. This was the home of the oysters, and God said, "My little children, you have no legs, you can not run; you have no feet, you can not walk; you have no wings, you can not fly; just open your mouths and your heavenly Father will feed you: you will grow and when grown you will furnish the wealth to build my church at Kinnakeet, North Carolina. That will be my miracle church."

The word was passed to the oyster buyers of Virginia and Maryland that there was an oyster mass at Cape Channel near Kinnakeet, North Carolina. They came to Cape Channel in large sloops and two-masted schooners laden with gold and silver. It was an economic miracle and a blessing that God sent to these impoverished people. The people of Kinnakeet, being a seafaring people, were amply prepared to meet the situation. There were at least fifty, two-masted schooners, about one hundred canoes and sailing skiffs at the Kinnakeet anchorage ready for instant use. The village front looked like a Norwegian fishing village.

Every boat that was seaworthy was requisitioned and placed in service. God showered his blessings upon them. The hour of their good fortune had struck in a land of impoverishment. With the rod of God's love, they struck the vast oyster rocks and abundant streams of gold and silver gushed forth and lined their pockets with needed wealth. Five years they worked, saved, and pooled their financial resources.

In the year 1885, they went to the mainland lumber mills and returned laden with lumber to build the first village church. All village activity was suspended. The people organized themselves in team work: one team unloading the boats on the Pamlico shore line, another team paired off using their bodies for horses and shoulders for wagons delivering the lumber to the building site.

The carpenters started immediate construction. They were happy in an air of complete love and harmony, continually shouting, singing and giving praise to the Lord for His blessing and continued care. The foundation quickly laid and beautifully designed and the structure taking form and quickly finished was dedicated to the Lord and was named Saint John's Church, in memory of the apostle of love. This church was a landmark for decades. Unfortunately, by the relentless power of nature it was partially destroyed and became unusable.

In 1962, a new church arose from its ruins. Kinnakeet was blessed by God, having erected to His glory another church, the Methodist Episcopal Church North, which is not united with the United Methodist Church.

In later years God moved in the power of His Holy Spirit and blessed the people by instituting the construction of the Assembly Church of God, which has become the rose of Sharon, the lily of the valley, the offspring of David, the bright morning star shedding the sweet influences of Christ in the souls and minds of His redeemed people.

The United Methodist Church and the Assembly of God Church are blessed in close fellowship and fidelity and friendship in Christ and are advancing the coming of God's kingdom of happiness of love in a growing magnificent way of truth and bonds of unity.

The builders of these churches were men of God under divine guidance. They worked for the fatherhood of God and brotherhood of man. They were aware that with the fleeting of time men would be drawn nearer together and become one in the unity of God.

What I have been taught by tradition and contact with these worthies of their vision of the Utopia that will exist when Christ returns in the new dawn, it thrills my soul to dream of the splendor of their vision that fills my soul of the life that will follow dying time. I am indebted to my father, Charles Williams, for the thoughts that I have in my mind of the beauties of the new day that will usher in.

When time will fold its wearied wings and lie perishing upon the beaten rock, I listen and lo! I hear the thunderings of the eternal morning as it breaks upon the prostrate form of past ages, while the earth trembling like an aspen leaf ceases its revolutions and àwaits the sentence of eternal justice. I look as I stand in the midst of the transitory scene and I behold the dark mantel that enshrouded the earth through the past ages, as it bursts asunder and the fragments roll back with the mist and like a surging billow recede into eternal darkness.

I look and behold the lightnings as they leap out from the hands of Jupiter: streaming, flashing through space, piercing the mountain tops, mingling its mutterings with the echo of the dying groans of time disappearing in the distance.

As we stand upon the threshold of a new dawn I look and behold kings, crowns, and princes in regalia dash out through space to share the fate of dying time.

I look and behold pride as it tumbles from its vaunting heights to be clothed with the garments it has scorned and despised.

I look and behold the bonds and chains of human slavery melting as they pass away like blazing meteors while the slave and the oppressed bathe their bruised and bleeding bodies in the balm of Gilead and chant the song of eternal freedom.

I look and behold virture as she stands out in the morning light of new dawn, with victory in her palm, while mischief expires in agony beneath her head.

I look in vain to behold the pale faces of innocence clinging to the ragged skirts of a widowed mother, crying for bread where its cries were not heard and its sufferings disregarded. I look in vain to behold the emaciated hand of the beggar extended to others.

I look and behold fever and all manner of diseases as they take their everlasting flight and oppression is banished from the scene.

I look and behold justice as she comes forth with the sword in her hand and commands the hosts to follow.

I look and behold the servant and his master, the rich and the poor, the ruler and the peasant, the high and low, the orphan and richly favored, the black and the white as they march forth together led by justice through the broad street of equality. I see them as they stack arms together and hang their harps on the willow tree and bow acknowledgement to the final conquest of the Galilan as He appears in their midst as the eternal light of the new dawn.

Camp Meeting

The Kinnakeeter born with an inherent desire to demonstrate his faith in God assembles in a fellowship of love under the benign influence of God's Grace. In the past ages at times, the Kinnakeeter during the summer would erect a camp ground at Jesse Gray's boat landing on the Pamlico Sound. This was a beautiful sandy opening of several acres under spacious skies and shining twinkling stars, a place where the heavens shed their sweet influences upon the beauties of one of God's chosen isles. The gentle breezy zephyrs of a balmy southwest wind bathe the place in the glory of God and the soothing night air was like the Balm of Gilead to sinful souls.

The Kinnakeeter on this site would erect a large tabernacle, wooden framed with a thatched roof, take his scythe and go in the marshes and cut bulrushes and spread them on the sand in the tabernacle for floors. They used planking for pews and pulpit, and hung oil lanterns by the hundreds to light the place at night. Seating capacity was around five to six hundred persons.

A prominent Methodist evangel would be the star speaker, dispensing the word in all its power. The people from Hatteras, Frisco, Buxton, Clarks, Rodanthe, Wanchese, and Stumpy Point were always cordially invited. The people from these villages would stop all their work for two weeks to attend the camp meeting. They came in great numbers, and used their sail skiffs for transportation.

The people of Kinnakeet would have the camp ground in complete order, laid off in streets awaiting the arrival of their visiting guests. Every man's boat would be pulled up the street to its approved place and propped so that it would not blow over if the wind got strong. Skiff sails were used to cover their boat wigwams. The camp ground was beautiful laid out in Indian design.

At the proper place a restaurant is erected and covered with large sails from someone's schooner boat. For breakfast, eggs and country smoked ham; for dinner, fried chicken and clam chowder of the most deluxe kind are served at the small price of twenty-five cents per meal. The soda jerker is present with his vanilla milk shake, sarsaparilla and root beer.

Everything now is in readiness for the meeting to start. An old-fashioned camp meeting is now under way. God is present leading the way. The saints of the Lord are working, extending their hand of love to the sinful, leading them to the Lord. The preacher in his sermons is reaching a high pitch of ecstasy. He pulls from the Throne of God a downpouring of Divine Love, and the glory of it seizes upon the souls of the elect of God and shouting and praising the Lord envelops the whole tabernacle and souls in great numbers are saved. The love feast lasts for two weeks. The visiting guests return to their respective villages carrying with them the young lambs of the Father, eager for the following summer to arrive so that they can return to Kinnakeet to a feast of joy and heaven come down and fill their cup with happiness.

A New Ship to Heaven

The revival meeting was progressing wonderfully, the holy spirit being poured out on all the members. A spiritual revival of unprecedented magnitude was being experienced. The last night of the meeting was highlighted by the witnessing of the faithful who were praising the Lord for His many blessings, love, and saving grace.

Captain Dave Pugh was explaining how one could get on board the old ship of Zion and land safely into the portals of glory. He used the local freight boat, the schooner, *H. P.*

Brown, which made weekly trips to Elizabeth City, North Carolina, to illustrate his point of view. His spiritual enthusiasm reached a glorious crescendo and he screamed out, "If you want to get to heaven all you have to do is to get on board of the *H. P. Brown* and she will land you safely to the city of Zion."

Gabriel Blows His Horn

Midsummer 1901, mosquitoe and flies darkened the skies at Kinnakeet; cattle, horses, hogs, and sheep roamed the village at will. They had learned that during mosquito and fly invasions the only source of relief was to go the Pamlico sound side of the village, wade out in the water until evening. They protected the exposed portions of their bodies by swishing their tails constantly, chewing the cud, and generally exhibiting a placid attitude of animal pleasantry. One particular day they came by the hundreds, wading out in the sound seeking daily relief.

In mid-Pamlico Sound the steamer, *Newbern*, was en route to Kinnakeet to ascertain the feasibility of making this town a port of call in order to make arrangements to establish a freight line to the Outer Banks. She was approaching the village via Cape Channel and negotiating as near as possible, but the shallow depth of water in the channel forced the steamer to anchor.

In the village all activity was at a standstill, no one knew of the *Newbern's* approach. Most every man was sleeping, getting rest for the night fishing. To attract the village that he was approaching the captain of the steamer blew his siren whistle which penetrated the heavens with a dreadful noise as thunderous tones of impending destruction.

Fear seized the minds of the people; the cattle, horses and hogs threw their heads in the air sniffing the breeze for some explanation. None to be had. Pandemonium seized them and in a wild stampede they marched bellowing, crying, kicking, and running through the village going eastward toward the ocean. When they reached the ocean they were forced to stop. One horse was so scared he plunged into the water and went as far as the off-bar. His body immersed, he turned and looked at the land, but stayed there two days until his fear left and returned back to his feeding grounds.

Anderson Gray was one of the outstanding church leaders, a saint of God; he was living in a spiritual belief of the imminent return of the Lord. He was waiting for Gabriel to plant one foot upon the sea and the other one on the land and blow his horn and declare in the name of the Lord that time shall be no more. Mr. Gray was in deep meditation, with arms folded and eyes piercingly looking at his stepson, Isaac, who had axe in hand uplifted to cut down a tree. Suddenly the heavens thundered in an unfamiliar sound.

Mr. Gray said, "Isaac, did you hear that piercing sound?" Then the second sound more ominous than the first, he said to Isaac, "Which way did that sound come from?"

The boy, with uplifted hand, replied, "Up there."

The old man said, "That is it! Gabriel has blown his horn. I have been waiting many years for that sound. Isaac, leave your axe at the root of the tree and we will now go home. It is all over."

The steamer, *Newbern*, had performed Gabriel's duty and knew it not.

KINNAKEET ATLANTIC ANCHORAGE BASIN

The Atlantic Basin is a basin formed by the confrontation of the ocean currents in battle for the mastery of the Atlantic Ocean along the eastern seaboard of the United States. These currents are the Gulf Stream and the Labrador Current. The Gulf Stream is the second largest ocean current. Only the Antarctic Current is greater. The Gulf Stream has its source in the warm waters of the eastern part of the Gulf of Mexico; these waters pass through the straits of Florida to become the Gulf Stream. The stream flows northeastward across the Atlantic toward the coast of Europe. The Gulf Stream flows as fast as 70 miles a day.

The Gulf Stream is partly responsible for making the climate of Great Britain and northwestern Europe much warmer than parts of North America that lie equally as far north. The Gulf Stream affects the climate of all nations that it borders. After the Gulf Stream flows through the Straits of Florida it passes the Little Bahama Bank. The Antilles Current, which flows northwest along the Atlantic side of the West Indies, then joins it, the combined current continues northward widening and slowing as it goes. The stream is about fifty miles wide and 3,000 feet deep, follows the Atlantic coast of North America. Sailors refer to a narrow strip of cold water as the "cold wall" which separates the Gulf Stream from the coast; this narrow wall of cold water is the Labrador Current.

At the southern edge of the Newfoundland Banks the Gulf Stream ceases to be a strong current and spreads out and becomes a drift of warm water that moves eastward toward Europe; this part of the stream is the North Atlantic Current. The Labrador Current is a cold ocean current that rises in the Arctic Ocean; it flows along the shores of Labrador to a point near the Island of Newfoundland where it meets the Gulf Stream. The influence of the Labrador Current is felt along the east coast of the United States as far south as Cape Hatteras, North Carolina. At this place it ceases its southerly flow. It continuously flows a southwestwardly course along the Continental shelf of North America at all times bordering the Gulf Stream.

At the point of Cape Hatteras, the Labrador Current and the Gulf Stream meet. At this place the Labrador Current puts up a heroic battle to predominate against the Gulf Stream. These two currents, one hot and the other one cold, meet and battle for the supremacy of the ocean. The two opposing currents meet on the Diamond Shoals in a majestic awesome display of natural power; ceaselessly the battle surges; currents, one from the north and one from the south, meet each other dealing crushing blows, the water spouting upward for 50 to 100 feet in the air. It is a brilliant sight to see in rough seas. The Gulf Stream flows onward northeast and shows no effects of the battle. Silently the Labrador Current curves seaward and melts away in defeat and joins the Gulf Stream in her victorious march to the northeast.

North of Cape Hatteras lies Kinnakeet and its Atlantic Anchorage Basin, a peaceful and restless anchorage for the sailing ships of all nations and a haven for tankers and steamships under attack by the German submarines during World Wars I and II.

Ships sail from Europe, Canada, and all parts of the United States north of Cape Hatteras en route to all parts of the United States south of Cape Hatteras, West Indies, Mexico, Central and South America, the West Coast of the United States, Hawaii, islands of the Pacific Ocean, Japan, China and all of the Orient. These ships, for speed and convenience, follow the United States east coast line sailing on the Labrador Current. Nearing Cape Hatteras, if they encounter a southwest, south or southeast wind, it becomes impossible for them to proceed any farther. They must await a shift of wind to the northwest or other northerly winds from some other quadrant of the circle. While waiting for a favorable wind so they can pass around the Diamond Shoals, due to the Gulf Stream current flowing around the Diamond Shoals to the northeast at a fast rate of speed, it is impossible for ships to make headway south against the current. Ships then seek anchorage in the Kinnakeet Anchorage Basin, anchoring close to land so as to be protected by the calmness of the lee of the land. At times there were a few ships anchored in the basin, but if the wind stayed on the south quarter their numbers increased to be very large.

I remember when I was a boy the wind during one summer blew from the southwest forty days and during that forty days two- or three-hundred sailing vessels, barks, barkentines, fully rigged square-riggers, two-, three- and four-masted schooners of all description were anchored in the Kinnakeet Anchorage Basin.

People that never saw the anchorage filled with ships can only have an artist's conception of what it looked like. During the night a brisk shift of wind to the northwest and in the early morning the ships, with all ouils spread, sailing in a southeast direction were a beauty to stir one's memory forever.

If the anchorage was filled in the late fall or early winter and the wind was cold and bitter and the wind was fair for them to go around the Diamond Shoals, they spread their sails and went in a southeast direction. You would then be treated with the beauty of the magic of the seemingly impossible.

The cool northwest air coming in contact with the warm air of the Gulf Stream produces a mirage that hovers over the sea like angels over a newborn babe that brings out the beauties of life. As the ships begin to fade from view and approach the mirage they begin to climb soaring in the air and the vast argosy of ships is a panoply of exquisite beauty sailing majestically in midair.

The anchorage has its horrors for sailors and ships as well as its conveniences. For the sailor it becomes a basin of deception, a trap which brings destruction to ships and death to the sailor.

In the days of the sailing ship there was no advanced technology of general and advanced knowledge of weather conditions as we have today; no airplanes keeping watch over storms and no radio to keep one informed as to weather conditions. Ships laden with cargo for southern ports south of Cape Hatteras, leave New York, Norfolk, and other northern ports in good weather but on arrival at Cape Hatteras they meet a moderate southerly wind so they go to the Kinnakeet Atlantic Basin and anchor and wait for a shift of wind northward. They are trapped and don't know it.

The wind calms to a warm southerly wave varying from southwest to southeast, therefore complicating the weather pattern. Nearby is a hurricane coming up the coast. High sea swells begin to roll in toward the beach. The ships pull in their anchors and hoist their sails and head out to sea, sailing up the coast as far as Whales Head Light. They encounter a sudden shift of wind to the north and start back toward Cape Hatteras. Off the coast of Chicamacomico the sea begins to wane; upon arrival at Kinnakeet the wind is beginning to breeze steadily from the south; the anchorage is rough and offers no protection. The ship is caught in the jaws of a fast approaching hurricane. The ship starts for Cape Henry and the protection of the Chesapeake Bay; up the North Carolina coast the ship soon encounters a raging northeast storm.

The captain scuds his ship south. The wind increases to hurricane force. His sails are torn to shreds and on Kinnakeet shore or the Diamond Shoals he lays his ship and himself at rest. This has been the pattern of lost ships and life for the past centuries. More ships and life have been lost in Kinnakeet Township than anywhere else in the world with the exception

64

of the Diamond Shoals, which is truly the graveyard of the Atlantic.

Whenever a ship was in danger from Cape Hatteras to Chicamacomico the Kinnakeeter was there to assist. Captain Pat Etheridge told his men on the Point of Cape Hatteras, when he was ordering them to sea, to rescue the crew of a ship that was in danger on the shoals in a raging sea. Someone questioned the wisdom of sending men to sea in such hazardous conditions. Captain Pat said the regulations said go, but said nothing about coming back. The ship was foundering, men lashed in the rigging. The rescue boat was manned, oars in place. A Kinnakeeter was in that boat.

The work of lifesaving and rescue of property is heroic and hazardous and at many times calls for the supreme gift. Kinnakeeters have died rescuing others. Whenever men are called from land-based stations or Coast Guard cutters you will find the Kinnakeeter there. Lifesaving is synonymous with disaster on sea or land. More Kinnakeeters are at the call of the Unites States Coast Guard for rescue or war service than from any other village anywhere in the United States in prorata of population.

SHIPWRECKS

I wish to introduce my chapter on shipwrecks as a preface to show the silent aftermath, by picture or photograph, the residue after a hurricane or storm of great power has agitated the mighty Atlantic to action and has passed and left a calm of destruction and twisted debris.

This photograph is a representative example of hundreds of ships that have been lost along the Kinnakeet beaches of North Carolina for centuries, and depicts by picture more than words can describe. Intriguing scenes like this are why the Kinnakeeter left his usual mode of work and engaged in the alluring vocation of dismantling and salvaging of ships, spars, sails, masts and other equipment. The salvaging of masts and getting them to the shipchandlers' market was labor of a stupendous magnitude. The masts were put on bedways and rollers of salvaged lumber and manhandled from the Atlantic ocean side to the Pamlico Sound side, and then towed by small sail boats up the Pamlico Sound, Albemarle Sound and Pasquotank River to Elizabeth City, North Carolina.

This picture is a gem, a pearl from the treasury of the familiar scenes of yesterday.

SHIPWRECKS

Shipwrecks along the North Carolina Coast made a profitable business for the working man. The Kinnakeeters would stop their fishing and oystering and devote their entire time to wrecking vessels and saving their cargoes for the lucrative monetary remuneration they received as salvors. A wreck commissioner was appointed by the Governor, each township having its commissioner. The Kinnakeet township commissioner was always a busy man; many vessels were constantly being beached. Salvaging wrecked property was a very steady industry. The wreck commissioner's fee was set by law at 5 per cent; shipowners and salvors usually agreed on a fifty-fifty basis of the balance that was left. If the owners and salvors could not agree on a settlement they would call in referees. Sometimes the referees would give the salvors as much as seventy to eighty per cent. If the cargo was of much value, buyers from Norfolk would bid in the cargo as a whole entity, and the salvors were employed by the purchasers to use their schooner boats and transport the cargo to Norfolk. It was the largest cash industry on the coast.

I want to write about some instances of shipwrecks that I am familiar with, and about ships trapped and lost in the Kinnakeet Atlantic Basin. I am not going into a detailed and comprehensive compilation of all wrecks in the Kinnakeet area, because they are all on the same pattern. When you are told one story you have the synopsis of all others.

Schooner John Shay

April 11, 1889, the schooner *John Shay* was trapped in the Kinnakeet Atlantic Anchorage Basin. Her loss was a saga of sea tragedy unparalleled in the sight and view of man. The Coast Guardsman and Kinnakeeter looked on in horror, pity and compassion, helpless to render assistance. The ship was caught off the North Carolina coast in the vicinity of Kinnakeet. Her situation was tragic. Her captain did everything humanly possible to keep his ship from foundering. He sailed off shore to ride out the terrific hurricane. The menfolk of Kinnakeet village gathered at the Big Kinnakeet Coast Guard Station, and volunteered their services if needed. The storm raged in intensity. The ship's sails were blown to shreds and torn to ribbons. The captain had no other recourse than to beach his ship. He hoisted the International Distress Signals, S O S, (Save our souls) and asked to be advised of the safest place to beach his ship.

The Coast Guardsmen knew that would be instant death for the crew and total destruction of the ship. The Coast Guard hoisted signals on the shore one by one, and gave warning to the *John Shay's* crew to scud her farther on to the south, pass through the inner slough of the Diamond Shoals, head west in the lee of the land and anchor in Raleigh Bay. The message was heeded. The Coast Guardsmen on foot and horse and the Kinnakeet volunteers followed the ship on her south course.

Heavy tidal waves crested and washed over the vessel, snap went her masts, the vessel helpless, fast disintegrated and went to pieces, the men on board clinging to the wreckage. More crested waves in quick succession swept the men in the open sea. All men on board drowned. That was a tragic experience for the heroic Coast Guardsmen in an hour of helpless desperation.

Robert W. Daisy

August 17, 1899, the Great Atlantic hurricane attacked the North Carolina Coast in great ferocity and destruction. The Kinnakeeters called it the August Storm. The name is extant to this day. Many sailing vessels were trapped in the Kinnakeet Atlantic Anchorage Basin and many ships were destroyed and strewn all along the Kinnakeet Banks.

One ship scudding South by Kinnakeet in a helpless condition went to pieces between Kinnakeet and Buxton.˙ Her wreckage washed ashore and one of her masts passed through Jennette's glade, the full length of Buxton which is about four miles, and went out through Peters Ditch into the Pamlico Sound. All of her crew perished.

A vessel anchored off Kinnakeet about two miles foundered and all her crew was lost. All that was ever seen of that vessel was her masts, tangled some way in anchors and chains that were on board and they stayed in that position for several years. Many ships trapped off shore went ashore in the vicinity of Chicamacomico and Salvo.

One of the ships trapped had more luck than the others. That ship was the *Robert W. Daisy*. She was sturdily built and beautifully designed, loaded with a cargo of coal. The captain reefed his sails and sailed off shore to ride out the storm. Three days he maneuvered his ship toward the land, tacked and went off shore. The hurricane grew in might, like a deadly rattler and ready to strike. She was weaving, tossing, feinting, changing her mind; she would vary from the northeast to the southeast, constantly increasing in strength, blowing so hard the waves were flattened.

The captain kept his ship off shore until her sails were blown to smithereens. Her crew was eager to beach the ship. The captain said no. Finally the crew took ropes and lashed the captain to the wheel, climbed and lashed themselves to the rigging. The captain put the ship on course for shore.

Going at railroad speed they passed through the eye of the hurricane, a dead calm.

The ship was caught in the vortex of three giant tidal waves, fifty to sixty feet high. She took the first wave. The captain maneuvered the ship and safely passed through the wave before it crested; the second wave coming in quick succession was passed through safely. The third wave caught his ship just beyond the off bar. The ship began to rise on the wave, reached the top and the wave carried the ship up on the beach, passed on across the island and the backwash receded to sea.

The ship was dry. The men unlashed themselves from the rigging, cut the ropes from around their captain. All the crew went over the side of the ship, gathered and formed a circle, and gave thanks to God for His loving kindness, and concern for saving their lives. They were carried to the Coast Guard Station, totally manned and captained by a crew of Kinnakeeters, given food and clothing, but best of all kind treatment and concern which is the way of life typical of the Kinnakeeter. Don't forget the Kinnakeeter was there.

Steamship Garland

During the summer of 1901, the night was stormy, sea rough, a thick London fog covered the ocean in the vicinity of Kinnakeet. The English tramp steamer *Garland* in ballast was lost in the fog, and opposite the Big Kinnakeet Coast Guard Station the steamer struck the beach. The captain blew his siren whistle continuously for hours.

My father and the other men of the village went to the oceanside to look for the steamer. I was ten years old and went along with them direct to the steamer.

The Big Kinnakeet, Little Kinnakeet and Cape Hatteras crews were standing by with lifeboat and breeches buoy, waiting for daylight to determine what course to pursue in making the rescue of the crew. The sea was too rough to use the lifeboat. The breeches buoy was used. The Lyle gun made a perfect shot across the ship's bow close to the mast. Crewmen on board quickly hauled the hawser on board, made it fast, and the breeches buoy was pulled to the ship. The crew was hauled to dry land without any loss of life.

Steamer Louise

I will now finish my wreck stories, and tell you about one of the most deadly and tragic that ever happened on the coast of North Carolina at Kinnakeet. It was never much publicized and not much attention paid to it, perhaps because it happened in time of war.

December 16, 1942, during the early morning the steamer *Louise* of Panamanian Register, loaded with truck tires and a crew of 13 men enroute from Norfolk, Virginia, to Panama, passed the Little Kinnakeet Coast Guard Station heading south, and passed the Station that same evening bound north. Darkness was fast setting in and it was blowing a storm from the northeast and snowing very hard. The ship quickly faded away in the darkness. The ship foundered and went to the bottom about one quarter of a mile from shore. Eleven of her crew were lost and two were saved.

When the ship faded from view, Chief Boatswain Mate James W. Scarborough, who was in command, put a steady patrol of men on the beach. Some were on horseback and some on foot, patrolling the beach both in a north and south direction. As a man washed up on the beach, a patrolman took him and carried him to the station.

The next morning I went to the Station, and it was a gruesome sight to see these men in the boat house stretched out in quiet silence. The crew were all Greeks.

Anna May

In 1946, during a Northeast storm, the fishing trawler *Anna May*, unable to ride out the storm at sea, was stranded on the Diamond Shoals off Cape Hatteras. It was a trying ordeal for the Coast Guard Lifesavers to put out to sea in a small lifeboat from a land-based Coast Guard Station on Cape Hatteras. They launched their boat from the south side of the Cape and braved the raging sea. Participating in the rescue were two Kinnakeeters, Richard Scarborough and Sumner Scarborough. When they finally reached the ship they found it sinking and going to pieces. The crew was unable to stay on deck and had lashed themselves in the rigging of the ship. Time a precious commodity with none to lose, they trusted in God, and in superhuman bravery they went as close to the ship as it was humanly possible, and as the crew jumped into the sea they were picked up by the lifesavers. The ship foundered and went to pieces in less than thirty minutes after the last man was saved.

For their bravery and heroic effort, Richard Scarborough and Sumner Scarborough, Sr., received the United States Government Lifesaving Medal. Another saga of human bravery, love and concern for his fellowman by brave Kinnakeeters.

Baxter B. Miller, Surfman

I wish to relate to you some of the heroic deeds of a Kinnakeeter, a surfman of the old Lifesaving Service of the ancient days. The official records at Coast Guard Headquarters show that Baxter B. Miller of Kinnakeet, North Carolina, enlisted in the Lifesaving Service at Cape Hatteras Lifesaving Station on November 20, 1890. For outstanding bravery and constancy to duty he went upward in rank to Warrant Boatswain. Miller served at Little Kinnakeet Lifeboat Station for about three years and was then transferred back to Cape Hatteras Lifeboat Station. After thirty years, two months and eleven days of honorable and faithful service he was retired. The Coast Guard records at Coast Guard Headquarters show that Miller was credited with assistance in saving approximately 300 lives, an incomprehensible feat, a feat to cheer the better sensibilities of mankind in saving life. Miller was the recipient of many medals for outstanding and heroic service.

On November 28, 1909, the German steamer *Brewster* was shipwrecked on the Diamond Shoals. In recognition of gallant conduct and heroic action in the rescue of the crew, Miller was awarded a gold medal by the Government of the United States, and a silver watch award by Kaiser Wilhelm in behalf of the Imperial Government of Germany.

On June 15, 1911, Miller rescued a man from drowning in the Pamlico Sound, North Carolina. In recognition of this outstanding bravery, he was awarded a silver medal by the Government of the United States.

Boatswain Miller, a Kinnakeeter of the highest and finest sensibilities and characteristics of the Kinnakeeter, has faded away in a halo of a glorious immortality.

Kinnakeeters to the Rescue

In August 1899, the Great Atlantic Hurricane, commonly called by the Outer Bankers the August Storm, was the longest and most vicious storm that ever struck the North Carolina Coast. A vast fleet of three-masted sailing schooners was trapped in the Kinnakeet Atlantic Anchorage Basin without any way to exit to safety. More ships were totally lost in the Kinnakeet area by foundering at sea or demolished when they were beached and more men lost their lives by drowning than in any other storm prior to or since that fateful storm.

During this dreadful storm the Kinnakeeter was a surfman in the crews of the Big Kinnakeet, Little Kinnakeet, Clarks, and Cape Hatteras Lifesaving Stations. They were men of high humanitarian qualities and acquitted themselves nobly.

73

I wish to mention the exploits of Surfman C. R. Hooper, attached to the Big Kinnakeet station, as an outstanding example of fidelity to the high calling of a lifesaver. His fidelity permeated the souls of every other Kinnakeeter in the Lifesaving Service at this particular time. Surfman Hooper was sent from the Big Kinnakeet Station on the south patrol on low tide as night was coming on. When he reached the section of the beach called the Hall Overs high water was beginning to make. The Hall Overs were covered with vast sand dunes, large and expansive, and heavily grassed with sea oats. With the rising of high water the violence of the wind increased and the going was tough.

A blinding sand storm was impeding Hopper's progress so he decided to go to the top of the highest and largest sand dune and dig a cave and get into it and stay until the high tide subsided. The sea increased in turbulence and enormous tidal waves swept the beaches; dune after dune eroded and disappeared. He was expecting his dune to erode and he would drown at any time. He knew the Kinnakeet Basin was filled with ships when the storm started to form and they would be scattered on the beaches at any time.

His watchful eye discovered a large three-masted vessel coming through the breakers in front of the dune that he was on. The ship was laboring greatly and was being torn to flinders in his presence. It was quickly torn and twisted to rubble and washed across the narrow strip of beach and disappeared from his view into the Pamlico Sound. Her entire crew perished and not a vestige of the ship was ever seen again. That was a night of lonely vigil, a night of horror.

He was alone on a desolate beach in a cave on top of a sand dune that was fast eroding with giant tidal waves constantly sweeping across the narrow beach thirty miles from the mainland and in midocean with a twisting, twirling monstrous hurricane, a cobra of the deep striking in all directions and destroying everything in its path. Water everywhere with no way of retreat, his cave was being filled by a torrential rain. In his dilemma of terror he put his faith in God, the Deliverer of

74

stranded souls, and offered a prayer to God to preserve him so he could continue to seek and help his forlorn and shipwrecked brothers on the beaches of Carolina for many years to come. God heard his prayer and sustained him and placed His hand in his and led him back to his station.

Only a brave stout soul such as his could maintain a composure under circumstances such as this. That is the quality of a unique race of people such as the Kinnakeeter.

For thirty years Surfman Hooper, who later became a warrant officer in the United States Coast Guard, participated in every instance of lifesaving which involved the Lifesaving Stations of Cape Hatteras, Big Kinnakeet, Little Kinnakeet, Gull Shoal, and Chicamacomico.

In January 1910, a great northeast storm was devastating the beaches of North Carolina especially in the vicinity of Cape Hatteras, and C. R. Hooper, officer in charge of Big Kinnakeet Lifesaving Station, kept a constant beach patrol active all during the night; his keen mind alert to the possibility of ships being wrecked in heavy snow storms. He sent Surfman E. F. Miller at 6 A.M. on a patrol of the south beach between Big Kinnakeet and Cape Hatteras lifeboat station.

In a blinding snowstorm Miller went about two miles south of the station when he suddenly discovered the schooner, *Frances*, being pounded to pieces by the relentless massive waves of the angry Atlantic like an untamed monster tearing its victim to pieces; her sails in tatters, her masts toppled, her spars and other debris being washed upon the beach. Miller, with much difficulty facing a heavy snowstorm driven by hurricane force winds, finally reached the station and reported his find to Officer C. R. Hooper.

Hooper immediately alerted his entire crew and dispatched them to the scene of the stricken vessel and with the aid of the Cape Hatteras crew combed the beaches searching for survivors, but no survivor or dead bodies were recovered. They did everything humanly possible to render assistance, but sadly the palm of victory silently eluded their noble efforts.

During the summer of 1915 a brisk wind was blowing

from the southwest and the small craft warning was hoisted. A three-masted vessel was in the vicinity of the Big Kinnakeet Coast Guard Station sailing on and off the beach waiting for a shift of wind to the northern quarter of the compass so she could pass the Outer Diamond Shoals enroute to the southern United States. In the late evening the ship came in close to the lee of the beach and about one mile off shore cast her anchor. During the night the wind shifted to the north and the sea got very rough. When the day dawned the ship was flying a distress signal; she was leaking and taking in water and in a sinking condition. Her crew had attempted to abandon ship but her lifeboat smashed and sank with her cable fastened to the stern of the vessel.

Officer in Charge C. R. Hooper mustered his men, ordered them to take Pat and Charlie, the big horses, put them in harness and pull the boat to the ocean side. Upon arrival they found the sea very rough but Officer Hooper did not hesitate. In his mind he saw a crew of men in desperate distress and ordered his crew to man the lifeboat, two bow oarsmen, two midship oarsmen, and two stern oarsmen; he ordered his most proficient surfman, Benjamin Scarborough, to use the megaphone and stand on the beach and direct the lifeboat through the slough and cross the bar to safety beyond breaking waters.

Officer Hooper manned the steering oar and relayed to the oarsmen the directions given by Surfman Scarborough who was stationed on the beach. The boat ready at the water's edge, at the opportune moment Scarborough gave the order launch off, hold boat in the slough. He watched the breakers on the off bar, and when the calm came on the bar he ordered pull fast and hard and cross the bar. Scarborough constantly gave the orders to row forward, row backward until the lifeboat was out of danger and out on the calmer open sea.

Just after they had crossed the bar a fast approaching wave came thundering in and Scarborough, through the megaphone, gave the order to pull fast and hard and meet the wave. The boat began to climb the wave and just as she

76

reached the top the wave crested and the lifeboat's stern arose visibly above the wave.

I was standing on the beach as a spectator and I said, "Gosh, the boat will pitch pole and empty the men in the sea."

That was a bloodcurdling, depressing sight. The wave came rushing shoreward leaving the brave Coast Guardsmen gliding majestically seaward like a stormy albatross hugging the bosom of the stormy deep.

The lifeboat arrived at the vessel's side and one by one the crew of the distressed vessel were safely placed in the lifeboat. They left the ship to her fate, a beautiful ship, new and on her maiden voyage and painted in a sheen of glistening white, and started for shore a place of safety and security.

As they neared the shore, Surfman Scarborough had the arduous task of bringing the boat and her precious cargo to land safely. Scarborough had to summon all his smartness and proficiency in seamanship and watch the tricks of an angry sea. He would tell them when to row forward, when to stop, when to row backward, when to pull slow, when to pull fast and when to ride a wave and finally he landed the boat safely on dry land. On the entire trip the boat had not taken in one gallon of water.

This safe action was due to the training and teamwork that Officer C. R. Hooper had taught and practiced with his crew in order to exact the maximum of efficiency that was needed in the Coast Guard Service. This kind of efficiency is why the Kinnakeeter is a lifesaver and a warrior for his country.

RESCUE AT SEA

Wherever a Coast Guard cutter is making a rescue at sea, you will find the Kinnakeeter taking an active part in the performance as an enlisted man or officer. This photo is a hand-painted artists conception of the Coast Guard cutter *Hamilton* making a rescue in a stormy sea. The helicopter in the picture is an integral part of the *Hamilton's* lifesaving apparatus making the rescue.

CONTACT WITH THE OUTSIDE WORLD

Kinnakeet was an integral part of Hyde County from the time of its first settlers until the year 1870. Swan Quarter was the county seat. All legal transactions pertinent to the life of the community was centered in Hyde County. This county became the clearing house for Kinnakeet to make contact with the outside world. Hyde County became the center of all outside activities of Kinnakeet Banks. People from Kinnakeet settled in parts of Hyde County and people from various villages emigrated to the Kinnakeet Banks. All commercial traffic and mail passed through Hyde County. This condition lasted until 1870 when Dare County was formed from sections of Hyde and Currituck counties. Change of counties and county seats revolutionized all modes of contact with the outside world for Kinnakeet. Their minds, trade and way of economic survival was oriented in Washington, North Carolina. This was quickly changed. Elizabeth City, Norfolk and the vast prospects burst upon the horizon of their vision and a new medium of contact with the outside world was established.

Mail service was established between Manteo and Kinnakeet by sailboat, which in that day was called the shad boat. They were built strong and of such design that they could be handled in most any kind of weather. People traveled to Manteo and made connection with other boats to Elizabeth City and Norfolk. This mode of travel was in time supplanted by small gas boats which brought the mail from Manteo to Kinnakeet. These boats were slow and most of the time were broken down and drifted helplessly. Travel to the outside world was markedly increased in efficiency and service by schooner boats carrying fish and oysters to the markets in Elizabeth City. A vast change was made by the plush accommodations afforded the public by the advent of the famous *Hattie Creef* and steamer *Trenton*.

Now our isolation is ended and we travel deluxe to all parts of the world.

The Kinnakeeter and the Coast Guard

In this book much has been said relative to the Kinnakeeter, and his relationship with the Coast Guard service. The Coast Guard has been his chief source of monetary income ever since the days of its first advent to the Outer Banks of North Carolina. The Kinnakeeter left his fishing, oystering and other industrial pursuits and enlisted in the Coast Guard service whenever the opportunity presented itself. The income was on a monthly basis and raised his standard of living, built his homes, fed his wife and children and gave his children the best in educational advantages, paid his college tuition and fitted him to compete in a contemporary world. The Kinnakeeter has been proud of the efficiency of the Coast Guard cutters, and has served on the smallest inland water cutters and the largest cutters of the North Atlantic weather patrol and on oversea bases from the North Sea to the Russian maritime provinces of eastern Siberia, rescuing life and property and fighting for his country and the free world.

To meet the needs of a new age for more endurance, faster and sturdier ships for the coast guard in time of peace and war, Coast Guard Headquarters designed and started construction of a fleet of high endurance cutters, smart in stormy weather, the last word in lifesaving technique and, in time of war, a miniature battleship.

On January 4, 1965, the keel of the USCGC *Hamilton* was laid in the Avondale shipyards of New Orleans, La. The

The new mammoth Coast Guard cutter: *Hamilton*.

USCGC *Hamilton* was named for the first secretary of the treasury department. This is the fifth USCGC to bear the name *Hamilton*. The first *Hamilton* was built in 1830. In 1853 she was lost with all hands, save one, in a violent Atlantic gale. In 1871 the second *Hamilton* was built in Buffalo, New York. She served with distinction in the war with Spain. The third cutter was a transferred naval gunboat, the USS *Vicksburg*, and renamed the *Hamilton*. In 1937 the fourth *Hamilton* was commissioned and on January 29, 1942, she was hit by an enemy torpedo and sunk in the North Atlantic. The fifth *Hamilton* is the first cutter of the Coast Guard's fleet modernization program and carries a complement of 166 men crew, is 378 feet long and weighs 2890 tons. During high speed operations she is capable of making 35 miles an hour. Her maneuverability and speed are designed to meet the Coast Guard's growing responsibilites in marine safety, marine law enforcement, military readiness and the scientific study of the oceans.

The *Hamilton* cost 30 million dollars. Every device in technological knowhow for service and convenience are installed in her sophisticated makeup. Her first crew of officers and enlisted men were picked for their proficiency and efficiency from the various stations, bases, and ships throughout the Coast Guard service.

For her chief yeoman Gerald D. Williams, a Kinnakeeter stationed at Cape Hatteras group, was picked by Coast Guard Headquarters as the most proficient and efficient yeoman to put the *Hamilton's* office in first-class condition for the reception of her incoming crew. Williams was transferred to the *Hamilton* prior to her commissioning and had everything in readiness to receive her crew of 166 men with their transfer papers and to file all transfer papers in their proper files as they came in. His proficiency was a quality of high competency, skilled and expert. His efficiency was a quality of ability to produce the desired effect with a minimum of effort, expense or waste.

Gerald D. Williams, in his office aboard the *Hamilton*.

THE KINNAKEETER'S WAR RECORD

Civil War

War, the scourge of heathen and civilized society, has plagued humanity since time immemorial. It rides a pale horse, and its driver is death. It has trampled with cruel ferocity the better sensibilities of every nation and watered the earth with tears of horror, and filled all lands with destitute widows and hungry orphans. It leads captive refugees fleeing from death to unwanted homes in strange lands. While I was writing, it was digging trenches in faroff Viet Nam and planting precious boys in the Mekong Delta. No land is immune from the foot of the pale horse.

Kinnakeet in its peaceful isolation and seclusion has been trampled, victimized and has suffered in the tragedies of bitter tears under the cruel foot of this merciless monster. However, every battle that has been fought has been a battle motivated for freedom. Freedom is purchased by a cruel price. Mr. Churchill said, "By sweat, blood and tears."

When our country needs the services of its young men, the Kinnakeeter is always there to fight and die to uphold the freedom and dignity of his country. Kinnakeet has furnished the Armed Forces of the United States more men than any other town or village in the United States, per capita of population. Fifty per cent of its manpower has been in continuous military service since 1915.

The war record of the Kinnakeeter started with the great Civil War. Federal warships cruising off the coast of North Carolina bombarded the village. The damage was minimal; one house was damaged. That was her baptism of war, a prelude of stirring events to happen. As the war progressed in the interior of the country, its cruel hand extended toward the Outer Banks. Fort Clark and Fort Hatteras were in operation at Hatteras, and occupied by an Indiana regiment of soldiers. The people were trapped and had no way to flee to the mainland. Riley Midgett started to flee to the mainland in his canoe carrying his family. Federal soldiers opened fire at him and it was said that he dived under water at the flash of the gun.

The Kinnakeeters enlisted in the Union Army as honor guards only, and were stationed at Fort Hatteras. They were used at times for duty outside of the fort. My grandfather, Evin Williams, an accomplished sailor and pilot, was used as a pilot to pilot Burnside's expedition through Hatteras Inlet and up through Pamlico Sound to capture Roanoke Island. A fierce battle was raging on the mainland and the home guards were ordered to go to the mainland and participate in the battle. The transport was brought to the dock for embarkation of the troops across Pamlico Sound. The troops were mustered out and placed under the command of Sergeant Lancaster Farrow, a Kinnakeeter. He marched his men to the transport. Upon arrival at the gangplank to board the ship, he gave the order, "Right face, forward march." Around the field they marched. With proper orders given, they quickly arrived at the gangplank again. Again the order, "Right face, forward march," was given, around the field they marched again. This movement went on in repetitive sequence for a long time. Finally the commanding officer ordered the men back to quarters. They did not go to the mainland.

Kinnakeet was placed under the terrors of occupation by Union soldiers. An Indiana regiment of infantry pitched their tents and placed the village under military control. They requisitioned for their use cattle, hogs, chickens, eggs and all vegetables the Kinnakeeter raised, leaving a starvation diet for

FORT HATTERAS, 1861

Fort Hatteras and the anchorage at Hatteras Inlet and a view of the camp of the 20th Indiana Regiment. This was taken from *Frank Leslie's Illustrated Newspaper*, November 9, 1861. It is a rare picture, which has been in my possession for ages. Due to the part that the Kinnakeeter played in the Civil War, this should be a scene of interest in his war record.

the village folk. They exercised harsh discipline and on one occasion killed a deaf man. The sentry gave an order to the man, Old Uncle Johnny Barnes, to halt. The old man was deaf and did not hear the order and was shot dead on the spot.

When the great Civil War was raging in all its fury, General Sherman in his march from Atlanta to the sea made the remark that war is hell. That is what Kinnakeet suffered under the occupation of Federal troops. Kinnakeet was at that time the most populous and wealthiest village on Hatteras Island, and it was seething with revolt. Her male population of military age being under duress from Federal troops enlisted as home guards in the Union Army and stationed at Fort Hatteras; and a part of the 20th Indiana regiment was sent to Kinnakeet as occupational troops. This occupation was terror for the village folk. No home was immune from their search for food and anything of value that they could steal. The doors of every home carried the scars and bruises from rifle butts where they were battered down in the search for valuables. The people put their savings in cans and buried them.

Spanish-American War

Cuba, struggling to free herself from under the cruel Spanish yoke, was putting up a heroic but losing battle. The American people with pity and sympathetic compassion prayed for peace in the island. The United States Government dispatched the battleship *Maine* to Havana on a goodwill mission. While there, due to some unknown cause, the ship exploded and sank; her crew drowned. Bodies picked out of the water were dispatched to the Norfolk Naval Base. Upon arrival of the bodies, mothers, wives and sweethearts of the dead assembled to bid their dear ones farewell, adieu, happy landing to the land of eternal rest.

The Kinnakeeter was there. A young sailor, Blivens Scarborough, one of the most melodious singers in the United States, was selected to sing the last farewell. He mounted the rostrum and in a pathetic tone he sang the song, "The Ship That Never Returned." Faces covered with handkerchiefs, tears of sadness flowed as rivers of water. The people coming to their feet shouting, crying, and an old fashioned revival of God's spirit was passing through.

Indignation and anger swept the nation, young men volunteered to serve their nation in the Armed Forces. The Kinnakeeters were among the first. Andrew Williams, Frank Williams, and others volunteered for the Navy. Ebenezer Scarborough joined the Army and served his country heroically from Cuba to the Philippines. The Kinnakeeter was there.

Boxer Uprising

In 1900, a Chinese Secret Society, known as "Boxers," led a rebellion against all foreigners in China, and against all Chinese Christians. Their aim was to kill all foreigners and Christians in China. There were 231 foreigners slain and an untold number of Christians. The German and Japanese chiefs of their legations were murdered. The Boxers laid siege to all foreign legations in Peking. England, France, Germany, Italy, Austria, the United States and other countries acted quickly in concert to relieve the siege. The United States sent Marines to China. The united force moved in on Peking and quickly put down the rebellion.

Ezekiel Scarborough, an enlised man on the United States Cruiser *Newark*, marched proudly down the streets of Peking upholding the honor of his country as a proud Kinnakeeter.

World War I

For many years the European nations were a seething mass of rivalry for power, commerce, and territory and foreign colonies. They sought balances of power, and began to form alliances, which finally resulted in the Triple Alliance, and

89

Triple Entente. Europe became an armed camp awaiting a spark of fire to ignite an unprecedented conflagration the like of which the world had never seen up to that time. In 1914 the murder of the Archduke Ferdinand in Serbia lighted the match that set the world on fire. Nations scrambled for national safety, quickly aligned themselves with the Alliance which seemed to give them the most protection. Germany and its allies were wreaking a bath of blood upon their neighbors. The United States, unprepared for instant action, began to look over its military hardware, bled Europe dry of its gold, offering its good offices for peace, rebuffed in each attempt. Germany became vicious and ruthless, decided upon unrestricted submarine warfare throughout the world. Down went the *Lusitania*. Hundreds of American lives perished in the English Channel. Horror gripped America. Finally in 1917, after three years of world terror, the United States declared war upon the German Alliance, called its people to a war to stop all future wars.

The Kinnakeeter responded to the call. Fifty percent of its available manpower rushed into the Navy, Coast Guard, Marine Corps and Army. Robert Farrow, a Marine, was sent to Europe and on the field of battle was severely wounded by shrapnel and was rushed to the Walter Reed Hospital, at which place he died in a few days. Blucher Scarborough, Walker Scarborough, and Bradford O'Neal were sent overseas and gallantly fought on the Hindenburg Line. Bradford, in a daring charge over the Hindenburg Line, was shot and severely wounded. Blucher was shot and a bullet struck him in the forehead, left its imprint, but did not penetrate the flesh. The Kinnakeeter on Coast Guard ships by the hundreds patrolled the sea lanes from America to Europe, fighting submarines and convoying ships carrying ammunition and supplies to the armies in Europe.

The Kinnakeeter was there in great force.

The older Kinnakeeter at home backed his sons and his neighbors' sons in their war effort by working in ammunition factories and Naval ship yards building and repairing ships.

Thirty men rushed to the E.I. Dupont de Nemours powder factories in Penns Grove, Pennsville and Deepwater in Delaware. This work was hazardous and very dangerous. They worked in blending towers, cutting houses, block breakers, and other places of a destructive nature. Sabotage was rampant. The night sky was frequently lighted by terrific blazing explosions, men bleeding, torn to shreds and dying. The high lights on the morning bulletin board gave the casualties of the previous night. It was a scene of constant death. The Kinnakeeter was there producing the necessary sinews of war, TNT, powder for machine guns, rifles and large howitzers for his sons to carry the war to a successful victory.

World War II

The Nationalist Socialist or Nazi Party in Germany came to power in 1933. Adolf Hitler had revealed his plans in 1925 in his book *Mein Kampf*. He urged the use of armed forces to remove the restrictions of the Versailles treaty of World War One. He called for rearmament and a union of all German-speaking people into a greater Germany. In 1935 Hitler established military conscription for all German men. Great Britain agreed to allow Germany to build an air force and navy. In 1936 Germany joined Italy and Japan in signing an anti-Comintern pact to oppose Communism. The three countries became allied in what was known as the Rome, Berlin, Tokyo Axis and in 1940 they signed a military pact. In the early spring of 1939 Hitler decided to attack Poland in September. All Europe was now ablaze. World War II was beginning in all its fury. Germany intended to build up a powerful empire by occupying territory to the East and South, then to overrun France. It expected to conquer the British Isles by an air assault. Finally, German troops would defeat Russia, capture the Caucasus oil fields, and unite with Italian armies advancing from Africa and Japanese armies advancing westward in Asia.

The people of the United States debated whether we

should enter or stay out of the war. The United States shifted its policy from neutrality to preparedness. It began to expand its Armed Forces, build defense plants and allow the Allies to buy military hardware on a cash-and-carry basis. In September, Great Britain being hardpressed, gave her fifty destroyers. President Roosevelt called upon the United States to become the arsenal of democracy, and supply war material to the Allies through sale, loan or lease.

Japan now controlled Manchuria, Korea and all the coast line of Asia to Indochina. All Chinese coastal commerce was in Japanese hands. Japan had driven the Communist forces back to the interior of Asia. In 1940 Japan occupied all of Indochina. Relations between Japan and the United States became increasingly tense. In the fall of 1941, a new Japanese cabinet took office and General Tojo became premier. They began planning an immediate war with the United States. Tojo sent Soburu Kuruso as a special representative to help Ambassador Nomuro to talk peace with the United States.

In 1941 the Japanese navy and army had completed their plans to bomb Pearl Harbor in Hawaii, and to invade Thailand, the Malay Peninsula and the Philippines. Early in November, Admiral Yamamoto, commander of the combined Japanese fleet set Sunday, December 8th Japanese time, which was December 7th our time, as the day of attack. Stealthily and secretly the minions of hell steamed for Pearl Harbor, about 7:55 a.m., December 7th on a beautiful, peaceful Sunday morning. The first bombs fell on Pearl Harbor; 360 planes attacked the Pacific Fleet while it was at anchor in the Naval Base and Army aircraft at Hickman Field and other nearby installations. When the assault ended nearly two hours later, the Pacific Fleet had lost the battleships *Arizona, California, Oklahoma,* and *West Virginia*; the minesweeper *Oglala* and the target ship *Utah*. The attack also destroyed 174 planes and damaged 4 battleships, 3 cruisers, and 3 destroyers. They had dealt the Pacific Fleet and Hawaai's air defenses a crippling blow, but they made a major mistake when they failed to return and destroy Pearl Harbor Naval Base completely.

The might of America's power, the pride of the Navy, lay in defeat at the bottom of Pearl Harbor. It was the most crushing defeat ever administered this country. The heart of America was frustrated and in terrible dismay. The fever of war was rampant. The signal of retaliation surged like mighty rivers on a rampage. President Roosevelt called December 7th a date that will live in infamy. On December 8, 1942, Congress declared war on the Imperial Japanese Government and authorized the President to employ the entire military forces of the United States and the resources of the Government to carry on war against the Imperial Government of Japan and to bring the conflict to a successful termination. All the resources of this country were thereby pledged by the Congress of the United States. World War II was now on—a war to victory or to death.

On that day of infamy at Pearl Harbor the Kinnakeeter was there, Vernon Miller, Boyd Gray and Winfred Whitlock. Now listen as Vernon Miller speaks.

"I am a sailor on the United States battleship *West Virginia*. Everything is peaceable and quiet, everyone resting, reading and writing letters to sweethearts and loved ones at home.

"Suddenly the fire alarm sounded on the bugle. Before the sound faded, the bugle sounded away fire-rescue squad; without intermission the bugle sounded general quarters. Planes flying low torpedoed the ship with an aerial torpedo. Between the time of first torpedo and leaving on way to Battle Station, we were struck by two more aerial torpedoes. The insignia of the Rising Sun was plainly painted on the planes. One torpedo bomber was flying so low that the pilot had to veer his plane to keep from hitting the ship's superstructure; one bomber plane coming so close to the ship that the duty officer fired his pistol at the pilot who was grinning a loathsome smile at us. Now we had been hit by seven torpedoes, several bombs, and strafed by machine guns, and now we were taking water in very fast. The bugle sounded orders to abandon ship. On one side of our ship the *Oklahoma* sank lying on her side, the

Arizona at our stern went down to a watery grave. The *Tennessee* moored at the docks inside of us, so we could not make the docks.

"Our ship was exploding internally. We knew we had to leave. Crude oil was flowing from sunken ships, filling the waters of the harbor and was suddenly blazing all around us. A blazing curling of the smoke of an inferno of hot hell was enveloping the ship. This Sunday morning became a pall of evil darkness. We had no recourse but to jump overboard in this burning cauldron of heat. We looked for an opening where we could dive through the fire so that we could swim under water to a spot of safety.

"Before we could jump a plane passed close over the burning ship strafing us boys on deck. About half of the boys were killed, some wounded, some in terrible agony, some passing out into eternity. One could almost feel their spirits hovering over those torments, awaiting their Eternal Pilot to carry them over the Great Divide.

"My pals and I saw an opening clear of fire and along with them I made a quick dive under the fiery water of burning oil and swam as far as we could and was picked up by a passing lifeboat. Some of the party was placed on board the boat, others clung to the lifeboat sides. We were carried to Fort Island. We were clothesless, left everything we had on board the ship. The clothes we had were soaked in oil. We were taken to the Naval Air Station and issued clothing. The clothes given me were a white sport shirt with pink flamingoes embroidered on the pockets, a pair of khaki pants several sizes too large, a pair of brogan shoes, one shoe a number 8, the other a number 10, and to make it worse both shoes were for the right foot. I wore that outfit for five days, over the crude oil suit that I already had on. Then our group reported to the Pearl Harbor Arena and were segregated in groups according to type of ship we came from. We slept on thin mattresses and had a thin mattress to cover with. The chow line ran continuously. They gave us a bowl of soup, and we returned to the line again.

"I went over to the dock and went on board of the heavy

94

cruiser *New Orleans* to get something to eat. While on board I talked with the Personnel Officer, related to him my experiences and asked him to place me on board his ship as a member of the crew. He told me that he was filled up with a full crew; however, the Executive Officer told me to stay on board. That evening we went to sea in company with two destroyers, submarine hunting in the vicinity of Johnson Island."

Pearl Harbor

On December 7, 1941, the day of infamy, Japanese bombers unheralded came out of the skies like the evil spirits of perdition on the sleeping American Pacific Fleet, hurtling death, fire, and agony on an unsuspecting friendly nation.

The watchful eye of an alert Kinnakeeter, Boatswain Mate Second Class Boyd Gray on board the destroyer *Dale*, U. S. Navy, saw the first bomber like a fast-falling star racing for Pearl Harbor. He manned the fire station and was wounded by shrapnel. His ship, undamaged, later put to sea and participated in the arduous struggle of driving the Japanese from the island of the South Pacific and Central Pacific Groups. Gray went with his ship and gallantly upheld the traditions of the United States Navy. A characteristic portrait of the Kinnakeeter in fidelity and constancy to his country's honor and defense. Gray took part in all the major battles and landings from Pearl Harbor to Okinawa, distinguished himself at Saipan, Guadalcanal, Phillippines and Okinawa. He received the Purple Heart and thirteen battle stars and many ribbons. A distinguished Kinnakeeter and an American of the highest order.

When the Japanese made their deceitful attack on Pearl Harbor, which bruised and bled the heart of America, Winifred Whitlock, Staff Sergeant, U. S. Army 24th Rangers, and a Kinnakeeter, was stationed at Schofield Field, Hawaii. Whitlock in charge of a detail of forty-five men was on duty at the fire station. The Japanese bombers came over in waves bombing and strafing. He saw ten of his men fall bleeding and

95

dying. Helpless he could look on only in horror, pity, and compassion. From Pearl Harbor, Whitlock went to New Guinea and fought the Japanese all the way to the Philippines. He fought in every battle of the South and Central Pacific. From island to island, he constantly month after month, and year after year, heard the heartbreaking cries of the dying and saw the agonies of the helpless in despair. Four long years he went through this ordeal in the service of his country. Wounded twice, he was awarded the Bomb Scarred Decoration. Twice he received this decoration. The last one an Oak Leaf Cluster. He saw his fellow Coast Guardsmen from Kinnakeet in action in the South Pacific and made this great remark, "They were unsung heroes."

Midway

Pearl Harbor had been bombed, the American Pacific Fleet practically destroyed, ineffective, and immobilized, and the sons of the Rising Sun had withdrawn into the dark vastness of the Pacific Ocean, now their pond. They were now masters of the Pacific Ocean. Their power was dominant throughout the vastness of the world's largest ocean. The Japanese had conquered the Philippine Islands, Solomon Island, Marshall Islands and all the islands of the South and Central Pacific Ocean isolated New Zealand and Australia and left them helpless.

Midway Island, one thousand miles northwest of Hawaii, for some unknown cause had not been attacked. The Japanese, taking swift advantage of the preoccupation of the United States in the European War Theatre, assembled a vast armada of one hundred ships, a large well equipped army, aircraft carriers and landing barges.

The Japanese naval war lords dispatched this invasion force to the Middle East. This great powerful armada of Asiatic might set sail for the Red Sea to enter into the Palestinian campaign and break the English resistance in Egypt and Palestine. The British had only a few ships left in the Indian Ocean. They were ordered to flee to Madagascar, and hide to avert disaster. The Japanese would have quickly defeated the British, who were already hard-pressed by Marshal Rommel's Afrika Korps, to take all of Africa, and the Middle East, and become the dominant power of the earth.

At this stage of the mysterious drama a strange thing happened. It is believed that the Divine Providence of God, through the oracles of His power, would not allow His timetable for the redemption of Israel to be foiled by the Japanese war hierarchy.

Admiral Yamamoto suddenly changed his mind and ordered the task force to turn around in the Indian Ocean and head for the West coast of the United States. If the Japanese had continued as originally planned, World War II could have had a different ending and the history of mankind changed for a thousand years.

The order to change course given by Admiral Yamamoto to his commanders was mysteriously discovered by some sailors of the U. S. Navy, intercepting the radio message and deciphering the code. The Japanese objective was to capture Midway Island, lure the American fleet remaining in Hawaii to sea and quickly destroy them by their powerful fleet. The Japanese fleet was the strongest aggregation of naval sea power ever assembled in the world up to this time in history. Cracking the Japanese naval code enabled the American commanders to gather a task force and surprise the Japanese at their own game.

A young Kinnakeeter, Vernon Miller of Pearl Harbor fame, was there on the U.S.S. *New Orleans* as it chased a disabled Japanese ship until she sank.

When the battle cleared, the Japanese had suffered the greatest defeat and sea disaster of modern times. Her mighty armada was no longer a threat to the United States.

The Islands Battles

From then on the battle from island to island was on for nearly four years. That is when the Kinnakeeter played his greatest role. Serving on Coast Guard and Naval ships convoying transport ships loaded with soldiers and marines, manning landing craft ships and Higgins boats, delivering the marines and soldiers on the beaches. The Kinnakeeter, known the world over as lifesavers, now became the transporters of the means of death to destroy people, and uphold his nation's honor. Kinnakeeters became the deliverers of men, materials, guns, tanks, rifles and ammunition to our marines and soldiers fighting on the beaches, in jungles, and in hand-to-hand conflict with the suicidal Japanese. Securing a beachhead for marines and soldiers, using Higgins boats exposed from enemy fire on shore and strafing by airplane, called for bravery of the highest order. The training in broken water by Coast Guard along the Atlantic Coast, performing rescue work, had made the Coast Guardsman a highly efficient specialist of rare ability in maneuvering boats in rough breaking water. The Kinnakeeter became a specialist of rare ability in the time of our national need.

Reginald Meekins

Reginald Meekins, one of the sons of a full-fledged Kinnakeeter, enlisted in the Coast Guard and was placed on the cutter *Liggett*. He served three years on this cutter in the Pacific area participating in all the landings in the Solomon Islands, and Marshall Group of islands, and performed heroic and hazardous duties in Guadalcanal and Tulaga.

I wish to write about one of the outstanding Kinnakeeters, Richard J. Scarborough who is lovingly called Dick by his neighbors, and who enlisted in the United States Coast Guard in 1923. When the Coast Guard during the War became an integral part of the Navy, Dick was transferred from a land-based station to the *McCauley*, a Grace Liner converted into a transport, debarked from New York to Iceland. It was attacked by submarines and went into Halifax, Nova Scotia. From Halifax they proceeded to Iceland and picked up the survivors of a Coast Guard cutter that had been torpedoed and carried them to New York; left New York and proceeded to Norfolk, Virginia; loaded supplies and troops destined to Wellington, New Zealand.

From Wellington they proceeded to Guadalcanal, invaded the island at nine-thirty in the morning. Everything proceeded smoothly, the troops were safely landed. During the evening the bombers came over and ran their escort of destroyers and cruisers away. This happened before they could land their supplies ashore for the Marines. Dick was in the first wave that landed on Guadalcanal. They lost one transport and one cruiser. They had on supplies for five days, ate their emergency rations. They ate coconuts, and coconut milk they drank for water, for several days. Dick was a Boatswain Mate First Class in charge of a Coast Guard detail which handled landing barges. He was transferred ashore permanently with Commander Dexter, in charge of the Coast Guard detail. When the Guard landed, they drove the Japanese into the jungle. They never received any return fire from the Japanese until about five days later when a sea battle started in the Savoil Island. We lost several ships. The airport was destroyed with all the planes on the ground by ship bombardment.

The American fleet, including the battleship *North Carolina* was called in, and they did much damage to the Japanese.

On one occasion they saw small boats drifting off shore and thought they were American survivors. Dick, in charge of a Higgins boat, went out to investigate and make a rescue. They went alongside one of the boats and found a man was lying on his face on a board in the boat. Discovering that he was not an American, but Japanese, and still alive, Dick reached to get his identification tag. The man came at Dick with a knife, but did no damage, just knocked his glasses overboard in the sea. The man was vicious and would not allow Dick to rescue him. He wielded his knife in a determined manner. Dick had to apply the law of self-protection, picked up a three-gallon jug and smashed the madman on the head. What happened to the man is one of the unwritten secrets of the sea.

Dick, after that episode was nicknamed "Scars," which is a symbol of physical suffering of seeing someone in anguish. Dick is a typical Kinnakeeter with a heart of love for his fellow man. Dick was there as a patriotic American ready to fight the evil one to the death. My fellow Americans, do not forget, if you were not there, Dick was, and it is for such we give glory. Dick received a Presidential Citation for his heroic service at Guadalcanal.

Guadalcanal

On August 7, 1942, the Allies began their first offensive action in the Pacific Area. Marines landed on Guadalcanal in the Solomon Islands. The fighting was bitter and control of the island seesawed for several months. In a sea battle near Tulagi, the USS *New Orleans*, a heavy cruiser, had her bow shot to pieces and went to Australia for repairs.

A Kinnakeeter, Vernon Miller, was attached to that ship. He was a hero of Pearl Harbor and Midway.

Coast Guardsman Ruffman Gray, a young Kinnakeeter serving on the USS *Alchiba* in Guadalcanal, went through the tortures of a fiery sea serving his country. His ship, the *Alchiba*, was torpedoed and sank in flames. When the order to abandon ship was given, Gray jumped overboard and was sucked under the stern of the ship by her churning propellers. He was rescued just as he was coming in contact with the propellers, and pulled to safety. Both arms severely burned and useless, he was rushed to the hospital on shore and, for further treatment, was sent to a hospital in the New Hebrides Islands. Incapacitated and unfit for duty he was sent back to the States. Gray received a Presidential Citation for bravery in action.

100

Roy Gray, a Kinnakeeter full of gay life and loved by all who knew him for his kindness and concern for his fellowman, enlisted in the U. S. Coast Guard and was stationed at a Lifeboat Station. Roy was called by his country to come to her defense. He was well prepared to perform the duties that his country had for him. He was a specialist in handling rescue boats on stormy beaches, and a master at handling boats in broken treacherous waters. The country needed him to man landing barges carrying marines and soldiers in invasion of foreign lands, securing beachheads for full scale invasion. Roy went overseas on the *McCauley*, a Grace Liner converted into a troopship and cargo carrier. He arrived in Guadalcanal and was transferred to the USS *Alchiba* and performed heroic work of bravery in landing marines and soldiers on the beaches. He was strafed by planes and bombed by bombers. Roy was on one of the ship's small boats and was tied up to the ship's gangplank afloat and ready to push away and leave the ship. Suddenly the *Alchiba* was torpedoed and quickly went down in an inferno of raging flames. To keep his board from being pulled under the water, Roy picked up a hatchet and cut the hawser and went away from the ship, and instantly converted the small boat into a rescue craft. Crewmen and soldiers were jumping overboard from the burning *Alchiba*. Roy was a coxswain in charge of the rescue craft and rescued the floating and swimming men until all were saved. Roy rescued sixty-eight men.

Vance Gray, another Kinnakeeter, a crewman of the *Alchiba*, had jumped overboard and Roy rescued him and pulled him aboard his boat. Roy stayed with his sunken ship until she was finally salvaged and returned to the States on the *Alchiba*, Roy received a unit Presidential Citation for stick-to-itiveness to duty under perilous circumstances.

Another characteristic portrait of the Kinnakeeter.

A Coast Guardsman, James I. Gray, was affectionately called by his people Jim Gray. A veteran of land-based Coast Guard rescue stations and a master of the tricks of the unruly Atlantic Ocean in the phenomena of broken waters, a sailor of wisdom and discretion, he was one of the few men amply prepared to serve their country in one of its most hazardous feats of landing marines and soldiers through raging billowy seas to establish a beachhead for the invasion of foreign lands. Gray, a versatile Kinnakeeter, was educated and received his experience in the tricks of broken water along the Kinnakeet Coast of North Carolina. When the Coast Guard became an integral part of the Navy in World War II, Gray was called. At Guadalcanal he was a member of the crew of the USS *Alchiba*. Gray was in charge of a Higgins boat, landing marines to secure a beachhead. Gray was with the first wave making a landing. He was strafed by Japanese planes and bombed from the air on many occasions. His ship, the *Alchiba*, was torpedoed and went down in a gulf of flames. The bugler blew the alarm "Abandon Ship." Gray jumped overboard and swam in circles until help arrived from the shore patrols. He lost everything he had. All he had left was the suit he had on when he made the jump.

Gray, in charge of a Higgins boat, soon became a lifesaver, a way of life dear to his heart. He took his Higgins boat and went to sea, rescuing survivors from the four heavy battle cruisers that went down in one night of battle. Gray made several trips to sea until all survivors were rescued. Gray received a Presidential Citation for devotion to duty, a brave Kinnakeeter, performing a double role, warrior and lifesaver.

The Philippines

The Philippines fell to Japan early in 1942. As the invaders approached the island the crew of an American naval ship scuttled their ship and took refuge on Corregidor, a rocky fortress in Manila Bay. General MacArthur declared Manila an open city and withdrew his troops to the Bataan Peninsula. The Japanese forced about forty-thousand prisoners to march seventy miles to prison camps. In the Bataan march more than half the prisoners died from starvation or maltreatment.

Thomas Midgett, a Kinnakeeter, was in that march. Not very husky he succumbed to maltreatment easily; weak, he was forced beyond his strength and beaten during the march. The International Red Cross investigated his case and reported that he died the horrible death of malnutrition caused by starvation. Another star in the crown of the Kinnakeeters' glory.

The War in the Atlantic

World War II in the Atlantic was reaching a climax for the Allied forces; France had surrendered, the British were driven out of Europe, planes and rockets were devastating London. Submarines were taking a tremendous toll of Allied shipping. The United States on December 8th, 1941 declared war on Japan. Germany and Italy, on the 11th of December, declared war on the United States. In a few days the United States declared war on Germany and her Allies. The American Atlantic Fleet and Coast Guard cutters were put in action patrolling the sea lanes between Europe and America hunting submarines, convoying merchant ships carrying the necessities and sinews of war to Europe as far north as Murmansk, Russia.

Almost all available Kinnakeeters on land-based Coast Guard Lifeboat Station were transferred to naval transports ferrying men and supplies to Europe and to training stations for amphibious landings.

The Kinnakeeter, a natural-born seaman, was very well adapted to operating boats in broken water. His services would soon be needed landing troops in France, North Africa, and Italy.

The British were fighting a seesaw campaign against the Germans and Italians in North Africa. In May, 1942, Rommel's Afrika Korps, aided by Italian troops, began a powerful offensive. The Germans captured Tobruk in Libya and dashed toward Egypt. The British army under General Montgomery took the offensive and rolled on to Tripoli and Southern Tunisia. Along with the British offensive in Tunisia the Allies planned an invasion of French North Africa. They hoped to force the Germans out of Africa. On November 7th, 1942, 500 troops and supply ships, escorted by more than 350 warships, transported Allied troops from the United States and the British Isles to North Africa. The first wave of American troops landed near Oran, Morocco.

The first Higgins boat landing craft loaded with men to reach shore was commanded by a Kinnakeeter, Evin Williams, a Chief Boatswain Mate in the United State Coast Guard service. As they approached land they were strafed and machine-gunned by low-flying planes; many men were killed on the craft. Williams' helmet was riddled by bullets and blew off his head but he escaped unhurt. The commanding officer of the Marines who were being landed jumped overboard and was never seen again. The ship made land and the Marines waded ashore. Williams turned his ship back to sea and went to his ship, which was a large transport ship, loaded his boat with Marines and carried them to the established beachhead. They shuttled men and supplies from the transport to the shore until the invasion was completed. Many other Kinnakeeters on Higgins boats were peforming the same duty at the same beachhead.

From North Africa Williams was transferred to Europe and in England was placed in charge of a patrol boat escorting ships across the English Channel. He came in contact with Warrant Officer Dewey Scarborough from Kinnakeet, who was in charge of a patrol boat escorting ships from England to France. They worked in conjunctive patrol duties and gallantly performed their duty to their country in great honor.

Many Kinnakeeters enlisted in the United States Army and were sent to Europe and made the first landing on the Normandy coast of France. Among them were: James Sawyer, Norman Gray, and Palmer Gray. These three men fought from the beachhead to the great Battle of the Bulge.

James Sawyer fought from Normandy to Austria and was

wounded three times and received a Purple Heart. Palmer Gray was killed at the Battle of the Bulge. He made the supreme sacrifice of fidelity and love for his country. Sleep, Kinnakeeter, your warfare is over. You have fought the good fight for freedom. Silently rest in the arms of Jesus and return with Him when He returns on wings of a new dawn, when the sword of war will be melted in the love of the fatherhood of God and the brotherhood of man.

Norman Gray fought bravely and gallantly and distinguished himself heroically to uphold the traditions of the American Army with honor.

America, France, Britain, and Russia were fighting desperately to vanquish the Germanic alliance. America was putting all her energies of strength, men, guns, ammunition, food, planes, and building millions of tons of victory ships, and building a bridge to hardpressed Europe. To protect this bridge of life America had to divert all of its destroyers, cruisers, battleships, and Coast Guard cutters to carry this precious flow of life, fight off the submarines and deliver this cargo to our soldiers and Marines in Europe, which practically left the shores of America unprotected. Germany, taking advantage of this desperate situation, dispatched a wolfpack of hungry submarines to attack American coastal shipping. Preferably their goal was to destroy the precious flow of oil from Venezuela, Mexico, and Texas to the oil refineries of Norfolk, Va., New Jersey, and New York. The lurking sharks of the deep congregated close to the eastern tip of the Diamond Shoals off Cape Hatteras to perform their dastardly, nefarious destructive mission of death.

Off the Kinnakeet Shore

America was unable to counteract and destroy the submarines. To divert ships from convoy duty was to court a greater disaster. The submarine warfare off the American coast had to be silently ignored. It was not to get to the newspapers. Our

105

soldiers in Europe were not to learn about the sinking of ships so close to home. Their morale must be kept at a high peak. If the soldiers knew of the great awesome warfare off Hatteras their morale would possible have sunk to a desperate level, probably the war quickly could have been lost.

The submarine warfare in all its fury raged off the Kinnakeet coast, ships being torpedoed day and night. Ceaselessly the roar of guns and window-shattering caused by the explosion of deadly torpedoes kept the nerves of the village folk on edge. The night skies were continually lighted by burning ships and oceans of oil in flames.

Ships coming from the south upon arriving at the eastern tip of the Diamond Shoals would change their course to the northwest. Submarine commanders like riders on the range would herd and chase these ships close to the shore line. The ships would get as close to the shoreline as possible, then head north hugging the beach so that the sea prowlers could not get close enough to torpedo them. On account of the shallowness of the water the submarines could not operate.

On one particular morning about twenty tankers and coastal freighters had come into the Kinnakeet Atlantic Basin close to the off bar. All of them painted in camouflage looked like a herd of prehistoric monsters seeking refuge from some mythological sea serpent of the Sargasso Sea.

The land-based Coast Guard stations from Bodies Island to Hatteras Inlet were turned into training stations for new recruits to man-convoying cutters and landing barges. Mostly all of these stations were commanded by Kinnakeeters. About 600 men were placed in these stations; the recruits were mostly Texans. Due to the submarine activity offshore, the beaches were put under intensive patrol. Hundreds of Texas horses were brought to the stations and the men patrolled the beaches on horses in pairs, fully armed for any eventuality.

The carnage of destruction and death off the Kinnakeet shore by the submarines was constant, the awesomeness of the conflict became more barbarous; submarine commanders would surface their ships and fire a shot across the bow of a tanker.

The crew was advised to man their lifeboats and row to the nearest land. After the ship was abandoned and torpedoed the submarine would draw near the lifeboat and machine gun the men at their oars and riddle the boat with machine gun bullets and leave the boats sinking. No wonder that man's inhumanity to man makes countless thousands mourn.

The Kinnakeet beaches were strewn with the debris from torpedoed ships, along with men, half-burned, crawling along its sands, half-crazed with pain and fear. The Kinnakeeter kept up a perfect patrol on the beaches saving men from boats that had been rowed ashore during the night.

During the last year of the war rumors persisted that spies had been landed on the Cape Hatteras beaches by submarines to work in conjunction with the submarines. Many ships were eluding the submarines by passing the Diamond Shoals at night and then heading northwest for the Kinnakeet sea basin and coming close to the shore line as possible. The German spies or agents would set miles of beach grass on fire to be used as a background to silhouette the ship, then submarines would draw near the ship and torpedo her. Many mysterious beach fires were constantly being started all the way from Bodies Island to Ocracoke.

While the guerrillas of the deep were busy ambushing and torpedoing ships, the Kinnakeeters were busy and alert on the beaches saving merchant seamen and giving them the best of human concern.

The terribleness of the conflict off the Kinnakeet shore deepens. Its tragedy becomes more sinister and darkens. It is no longer a war of destruction. It has become a war of tragic sport, human flesh, blood and cringing fear to satiate the enjoyment of the sharks of the deep. Tankers and freighters are torpedoed and sink beneath the waves. Their crews are allowed to get on rafts and man their lifeboats and drift and row around in circles. The hungry wolves of the deep surface and taunt and play tragic death with the sailors floating around with nowhere to go. The hunter herds them like a sheep-herding dog and fires streams of death into their hungry, despairing bodies and souls and butchers them with a gloat of laughter. All night their guns flash and light the eastern skies. Houses and windows shake and rattle from the percussion of their dastardly noise. Early morning and all day the cannonading continues. Shelling of helpless humanity in small boats and on rafts is a grinning and welcome sport to the blood-hungry gladiators of the deep. This kind of warfare goes on day and night with no relief in sight. Weeks, months and years the unrestricted reign of death wreaks its vengeance upon innocent humanity.

The Kinnakeeter is constantly patrolling the beaches, seeking to find some lucky straggler who may have reached shore during the night. Occasionally a boat is found loaded with survivors and given a new start in life.

Joe Williams, a Coast Guard patrolman, a Kinnakeeter on duty on the beaches in the darkness of night, suddenly came upon a small boat loaded with men who had drifted for many days and were shelled many times by a surfaced submarine. Some of the men were wounded and near death. All of them were Greeks and he could not understand their language. He signaled to them by sign language to follow him. He carried them to the Little Kinnakeet Coast Guard Station where they were no longer the object of deadly sport but recipients of the blessing of the brotherhood of man. Many boats washed ashore laden with the precious flotsam of the sea.

The steamship *Marore* was torpedoed about seven miles north of Diamond Shoals off the Kinnakeet beach. The crew was allowed one hour to abandon ship, man their lifeboats and leave the vicinity of the ship. With thunderous tones the torpedo struck the ship. Quickly the ship disappeared beneath the waves. Waters agitated by death and cruelty, the lifeboats loaded with cargoes of human life were shelled. Men dying, praying and crying with extended arms, placing themselves in the care of their Heavenly Father went out into eternity a victim of man's evil and stupidity. One lifeboat was fortunate. She had a sail and mast on board. They hoisted their sail in the darkness and quickly disappeared from the carnage of death and beached their boat in hollering distance of the Big Kinnakeet Coast Guard Station. Every man was saved, rescued by the Kinnakeeter who was there ready to heal the wounds and rescue the dying.

The steamship *Alexandria* en route from South America or some port of the United States came cautiously north along the Atlantic seaboard of the United States, eluding the black panthers of German cruelty, rounded the spit of the Diamond Shoals and came close in shore seeking the protection of the Kinnakeet Atlantic Anchorage Basin. It was torpedoed. Her crew managed to get into their lifeboats and became targets of the prowlers of desperation and mockers of justice. Their boats were shelled by the marauding raiders and sank. Every man on these small boats was killed by machine guns and their bodies eaten by man-eating sharks.

That was a night of terror for the village folk. In the dawn of the early morning two young Kinnakeet boys, Gib Gray, Jr., and Wilbur Gray rushed to the beach and found one of the boats of the steamship *Alexandria* that had just washed ashore. That lifeboat was the last boat that came ashore during the war. Her crew had been killed by the evil spirits of Hitler's wrath upon mankind.

These denizens of the nether world of perdition dyed the waters off Kinnakeet coast with a bath of blood. For two years the Atlantic ran red with the blood of men that go down to the sea.

The boat was riddled and pocked with bullet holes from stem to stern, a silent evidence of the gruesome tales of death on the high seas.

On a Sunday afternoon my wife, Ianthia Williams, and Charles Williams III, my grandson, and I went to the beach and took a photograph of the boat and I am including it in this book as the last vestige that remains on Kinnakeet of the most destructive war of all times.

The memory of the brave men who died off the shores of Kinnakeet, and the conern of the Kinnakeeters for humanity in perilous times and conditions, material and spiritual will never die.

Lifeboat of *S.S. Alexandria*, W.W. II

Korea

During the Korean war Kinnakeet was efficiently and highly represented by the enlisted men in the United States Coast Guard service patrolling the coast of Korea. There is not anything of heroic duty or bravery performed to write about. They were there on duty.

Vietnam

The Kinnakecter has been very prominent in the long conflict. They were there in large numbers serving on Coast Guard cutters patrolling the Vietnamese coastline, the Mekong river and anywhere that their services were needed.

All military men from Kinnakeet serving in Vietnam have been Coast Guardsmen, with the exception of Clayton Brothers III who enlisted in the air force and stayed in Vietnam his entire enlistment and did brave work and went through many narrow escapes and harrowing ordeals and acquitted himself with extreme bravery.

And George Wesley Basnett, whose grandfather, George Williams, was a Kinnakeeter and a Methodist preacher, was there. His mother, Grace Basnett, is a saintly woman who livoo in awe and adoration of her Creator. Young Basnett has inherited the qualities of life that make him a Kinnakeeter of the highest order. Mr. Basnett enlisted in the air force at Campbell, Kentucky, in 1965 and was placed in the 101st Airborne Division and trained as a parachute jumper. In 1968 the 101st Division was sent direct to Vietnam to participate in a dreadful jungle battle of fierce dimensions that was raging. The airplane that he was attached to went into immediate action and her parachute crew made the jump and slowly drifted down into the jungle and came under intense fire from a band of guerrillas. His comrades were shot and bayoneted to the last man, leaving Basnett alone and surrounded by hostile forces. He hid into the underbrush of the jungle and could see the

111

Viet Cong with drawn bayonets making a thorough search of the jungle for any survivors. He eluded them until they retreated into the depths of the jungle. In a few days helicopter crews came overhead and he signaled to them and was rescued and carried to safety.

For his heroism in this jungle battle Mr. Basnett was greatly honored by his country.

From the Department of the Army:

This is to certify that the Secretary of the Army has awarded the Army Commendation Medal to Specialist George Wesley Basnett, United States Army, for heroism in the Republic of Vietnam, 21st of May 1968 101st Airborne Division, parachute jumper.

In June 1968 during the Tet offensive in a hard fought battle the 101st Airborne Division was called upon for instant help and many men parachuted to the designated place and they instantly came under murderous fire from the North Vietnamese. Tragically the battle was not going well with the American parachuters. Mr. Basnett was Chief Communications Officer from the battle front with the Base Commander and was unable to get his message through for help. He crawled, walked, and ran the gauntlet of machine gun and rifle fire and finally made the Base alive and unhurt and brought help to his beleaguered and desperate brave comrade airmen. For this brave act beyond the call of duty he was signally honored by The President of the United States of America.

The United States of America.
To all who shall see these presents, Greeting.

This is to certify that the President of the United States of America, authorized by order 24, 24th August, 1962, has awarded the Bronze Medal to Sergeant George Wesley Basnett, for Meritorious Achievement in ground operations against hostile forces in the Republic of Vietnam, during the period 26th June, 1968. Given under my hand in the City of Washington, the 18th day of July, 1968.

George's father, Raymond Basnett, distinguished himself in World War II; 28 months he served on a cargo attack landing craft and fought from Guadalcanal to Okinawa. He started out with a fleet of 36 vessels and during the 28 months all the fleet was destroyed except the ship that he was attached to. He received the Unit Presidential Citation for devotion to duty.

George Wesley Basnett, genealogically, is a direct descendant of Caleb Williams, one of the first men shipwrecked on the Kinnakeet beach and one of the first to make the Kinnakeet Indian village his home. George is proud of his ancestry. He is now stationed at Tampa, Florida, under Headquarters Strategic Command, ready and trained at any moment to be sent to any hotspot of the world.

George has magnificently suffered the ordeal of seeing his comrades shot, stabbed and dying; loneliness, homesickness, being away from loved ones and is now living a live lion for his Heavenly Father, and a living hero in the service of his country.

George, you have faithfully carried out the qualitative enhancement of the uniqueness of the Kinnakeeter.

This is a photo of George Wesley Basnett, standing beside his citations.

KINNAKEET INVADED
AS NAVY MOVES TO PROTECT CAPE HATTERAS

The U. S. Government, cognizant of its unpreparedness during World War II to protect the United States coastal waters off Cape Hatteras from the depredations by German submarine boats, sent an expeditionary force in 1955 to Cape Hatteras to provide some degree of protection.

The waters off Kinnakeet and Cape Hatteras have been the scene of many bloody fights. Now Cape Hatteras is the nation's secret bastion of tremendous strength against future wars of underwater activity off the sea lanes of Cape Hatteras, the sea lanes off the Cape Hatteras Coast, which in two world wars have suffered in awesome silence the most destructive and barbarous warfare ever perpetrated anywhere in the Western Hemisphere. At long last they are to be offered some measure of protection.

Recently the harbor of this most picturesque village on the Outer Banks, located midway of Hatteras Island, was the scene of an unparalleled Seabee invasion. The Navy moved in on a sleeping Cape Hatteras with as much secrecy and surprise to the natives as the Icelandic people experienced in World War II when they were taken over. As the gray fingers of dawn brushed aside the dark wings of night, a flotilla of Naval craft approached Kinnakeet Harbor. People from all sections of the village gathered to watch the incoming procession. Speculation as to the impending dire forebodings of the future was rampant. The landing craft approached the docks, made fast, and rapidly began discharging their cargoes of giant cranes, sand-diggers, tractors and other heavy equipment.

The natives, watching every movement with intense interest, prophesied great things for the village. Their predictions, however, included dread thoughts for the future. Others worried that the heavy equipment would mar the beauty of the docks and the surrounding landscape.

Manned by Seabees, the giant rolling stock, so much an integral part of modern warfare, moved off for a point near Cape Hatteras, their engines screaming and roaring like some prehistoric animal and their widespread treads grinding down with impartial ferocity the trees, underbrush, and marsh grasses which stood in their path. Behind was left the memory of a placid harbor.

Here are six small pictures, showing a part of the naval flotilla of landing craft that invaded the sleeping village of Kinnakeet in 1955 to build a secret bastion of defense against enemy submarines as a protection to shipping off the sea lanes of Cape Hatteras. This was a task force which landed to establish a defense point somewhere in the vicinity of Cape Hatteras. Now the installations are as much a secret to the public of the United States as the invasion of Kinnakeet was.

Naval Invasion, 1955

117

POETRY

In this book I have been portraying the Kinnakeeter as a seeker after knowledge and education, as a searcher in the quest for the spiritual values of life, as a lifesaver and a warrior. Now I want to present the Kinnakeeter as a poet who writes and expresses himself with imagination, power and beauty of thought and reveals the inner recesses of his soul with originality in expressive language.

Kinnakeet's poet laureate was Charles Williams, Sr. Not many of his poems are extant to this day. All of his writings, imaginative, historical, and poetic were lost in the great 1944 hurricane, which destroyed his home and all of his belongings.

However I had in my possession the poem which he prized the highest of all, "The Lost Colony of Roanoke Island," which I now wish to be printed and become a part of this book.

The most pathetic and soul touching was his poem, "The Wreck of the *John Shay*." This poem was written in a saga of disaster, a search for a haven of safety and ends in the tragedy of death. This poem was lost along with his other writings in the great storm.

Other Kinnakeeters have been proficient in poetry, notably Dorcas Williams and Virginia Scarborough who have contributed very much to the poetic soul of the Kinnakeeter.

I wish to have my own poem, "When a Christian," to become a part of this book.

Many years ago the Pepsi Cola Company offered a first and second prize for the best jingle on the word Pepsi Cola. Charles Williams, Sr., won the first and second prizes. His verse for the first prize is as follows.

Give PepsiCola to your girl.
There's nothing beats it in the world.
Pop the question while she drinks.
She will answer yes before she thinks.

For the second prize:

If PepsiCola had been made
And Eve had given to Adam
He would not have eaten the forbidden fruit
And neither would the madam.

The Lost Colony of Roanoke Island

By C. T. WILLIAMS, SR.

Locked secure in the bosom of time lies a mystery
Of a colony born on a beautiful Isle,
Unsolved by the legends of savage tradition
Where crowns are not worn, and where liberty smiles,

Behold the frail craft as they bound o'er the billows,
Lashed by the rude waves and confused by the storms,
While seraphs unseen hovered round to protect them,
To guide them through safely and protect them from harm.

Determined to go and accomplish their Mission,
They trusted in God and fought the rude storm.
On a beautiful Isle on the strand of Carolina
A nation was planted, a Daughter was Born.

Borne on the wings of the stork from the forest
They greet the White Doe, the first English Child,
Where the Scuppernong grapes and the Violets entangle
Bedecking the brow of the Beautiful Isle.

The savage lay sleeping, his tomahawk buried,
His arrow returned to its quiver at night,
Found when he awoke in the dawn of the morning
What for refuge the Britons had taken their flight.

The Colonist nurtured with hope and ambition,
Moved whither no mortal has yet ever known.
They left their rude huts and daringly ventured
Midst wild beast and savage the forest to roam.

Fearless and brave, yet wise and precautious,
For safety resolved it was prudent to flee.
They left us no record nor clue to their going
Save one silent word which they carved on a tree.

Undisturbed and in silent repose they are sleeping
A Mantel of mystery tucked over their head
To remain till the earth shall surrender its treasures
They then will come forth with the world's honored dead.

In the great Conflagration which the world is approaching
When Empires and Kingdoms shall burn as a Scroll
And the archives of unwritten history is opened
Not till then will the fate of the Colony be told.

Avon, North Carolina

August, 1905

122

When a Christian

C. T. Williams II

A man is not thinking mean, when he is a Christian.
His thoughts are mostly clean, when a Christian.

He doesn't knock his fellow men,
Or harbor any grudges then,
A man is at his finest, when a Christian.

A man isn't plotting schemes, when he is a Christian.
He is busy with loving dreams, when a Christian.
His creed is to do the best he can,
A man is mostly man, when he is a Christian.

The rich are comrades to the poor, when they are Christians;
All brothers of a humble Christ, when they are Christians,

The Christian boy, with kite and string,
Can chum with millionaire and king.
Vain pride is a forgotten thing, when they are Christians,

A man has no time to hate, when he is a Christian,
He isn't eager to be great, when a Christian.
He isn't thinking thoughts of self,
or of worldly goods upon the shelf,
He is always just himself, when a Christian.

A woman gets a chance to dream, when she is a Christian
She learns the beauty of life's stream, when she is a Christian.
She can wash her soul in God's free air,
That isn't foul with selfish fare, when she is a Christian,

Men and women are glad to be a friend, when Christians,
A helping hand they will always lend, when Christians,
They are brothers and sisters of a stream that's fine,
They come real close to God's design, when they are Christians.

MODERN KINNAKEET

Avon

Kinnakeet was Kinnakeet to the Indian, Kinnakeet to the outside world and Kinnakeet to the Kinnakeeter. Kinnakeet was the first name applied by the United States Postal authorities as the official name of the Post Office at Kinnakeet on December 4, 1873. Damon Meekins was the first Postmaster. The name was changed to Avon, March 22, 1883, with Euphemia C. Williams as Postmaster. Avon got its name from Stratford on Avon, a town in Warwickshire, England, on the Avon River, the birth and burial place of Shakespeare. Truly the place where the elite and upper class of the world lived, died and were buried. The following is a list of names of the Postmasters that have served Kinnakeet for the last one hundred years:

Damon G. Meekins
Ignatius H. Scarborough
Harris F. Miller
Andrew W. Price
Mrs. Euphemia C. Williams
Cyrus R. Hooper
Howard S. Gray
C. B. Lincoln
Charles T. Williams
Melvinia F. Scarborough
Mrs. Dorcas Meekins
Velma W. Barnette

Kinnakeet has always enjoyed a population explosion, and due to economic reasons has moved in small colonies to other villages and towns and carried with them the uniqueness and characteristics of the upper class of citizens. Full of ambition, forward and easily adapting to a new environment, they make a success in their new homes.

Many years ago Buxton on Cape Hatteras was underpopulated. The Millers, Grays, Williamses and Scarboroughs immigrated to Buxton and built their homes. They assimilated themselves with the Buxton people and became political, social and church leaders. A colony of Midgetts, Grays, Millers, and Williamses settled in Elizabeth City, N. C. They carried their spirit of public pride and became church leaders and business men. Many Kinnakeeters have moved to Chesapeake, Norfolk, and Virginia Beach, Va., and have entered the stream of public life acquiring handsome paying positions and lucrative businesses of their own. They have become church workers, Sunday School teachers, and valued citizens. Three families of Williamses, O'Neals, and Scarboroughs have settled in Manteo, N. C., and established a Little Kinnakeet in the environs of the city, and carried the attributes of the Kinnakeeter with them, and are now enriching the political, social and church life of the town.

Wherever you find him he is still a Kinnakeeter. Kinnakeet is his first allegiance and they keep the traditions deep by fellowship with relatives left at Kinnakeet by a yearly homecoming in fellowship and love. Kinnakeet is now enjoying an expansive tourist boom, and an addition of new citizens of a high middle-class order. The Goldberg brothers, George and Ed, brilliant and highly sophisticated real estate operators, have purchased a sizable tract of land, subdivided it in lots and named it the Hatteras Colony. They are bringing in a high class of people, ladies and gentlemen, doctors, lawyers, writers, preachers and people of civic pride. They seem to be screening their settlers, just bringing in the finest of folk. They do not cater to the honkytonk class at all. They deserve the plaudits and credit of the Kinnakeeters, which they get.

126

KINNAKEET HARBOR, NOW
CALLED AVON HARBOR.

The people they bring in are civic-minded and the best of citizens. They visit and participate in the village church life. They are interested in the welfare of the village and in every avenue of its life. They are members of the Volunteer Fire Department and Anglers Club.

We are proud of our new citizens, the Smiths, Trueloves, Jennettes, Fletchers, Beckhams, Goldbergs, Younces, Outtens, Lambs, Lilleys, Fredericksons, Saunders, Gregorys, Whitehursts and a host of others.

One of the most attractive places of interest of modern Kinnakeet is Kinnakeet Harbor, now called Avon Harbor, owned and operated by the Corps of Engineers of the United States Army.

It is a harbor of scenic placidity where tourists can visit and view nature draped in its best. The beauties of sunset at Avon Harbor are one of the rare gems of nature. When the sun is setting beyond the western skies in her triumphal march through the heavens, it meets the placid waters of the Pamlico Sound and begins to kiss the water. It gently grows pale, and seemingly drips dews of liquid fire in the water and silently dips beneath the waters in a watery grave. It paints the skies with a glow of evening with all the colors of a brilliant rainbow. This is a pearl of nature that will linger in the mind of the viewer forever. One stands in awe of his Creator and exclaims, "How great thou art!" Many people come from all ranks of life and distant places in increasing numbers to take a photographic view of this display of natural beauty.

This harbor is a mecca for the sportsman who is interested in fishing with rod and reel in the Pamlico Sound and the fabulous fishing hole of the Cape Channel. Kinnakeet, from antiquity being a fishing village, shows in a glowing perspective some of the priceless pictures of the old set net days, men mending their nets and living a carefree life of peace.

Kinnakeet is uniquely situated geographically on Hatteras Island as the home and habitat of the fish kingdom. So much so that the painted sign on the Kinnakeet pier says, "If they swim they are here."

The Kinnakeet basin has been filled with fish ever since God created the earth. Fish was the main source of food for the Kinnakeet Indians and the first settlers. In the days of the New England fishing smack fleet, propelled by sail along the Kinnakeet coast line, the basin was picturesquely filled with them and they carried back to Boston and other New England ports thousands of tons of choice fish.

The Kinnakeeter, a seaman of quality, has for ages rowed his dory through the treacherous sea breakers on the off bar and set his nets by drop netting or making a semicircle and by pulling his net by hand to the beach. For surf-casting the Kinnakeet beaches are unequalled.

Red drum, a favorite of surf-casters, are abundant. Spot, sea mullet, blue fish, trout and every variety of fish can be found.

Modern Kinnakeet has an Atlantic fishing pier, operated and partially owned by an enterprising Kinnakeeter, Dewey Scarborough, whose hospitality to the fisherman is helpful and instructive. People from all over the world come and fish from this pier and usually carry home with them cans filled with fish, filleted, ready for the frying pan. This pier is an attractively designed structure for the enjoyment of the tourist and fisherman, also a place of pleasure for the visiting public. It enhances the portrait of the Kinnakeeter in his concern for the pleasantries of life of his guests and visitors. If you are not a fisherman come to the pier and rest. Come in the early morning, breathe fresh unpolluted air and view the beauties and glories of a rising sun. Come in the evening and see the halo of glory surrounding a sunset as she dips and fades in the Pamlico Sound.

The early Kinnakeeter stranded on a beautiful isle, and in primitive seclusion and inaccessible only to the adventurous, and, with no way to return to his native land, had to settle down and adapt himself to the cruel vicissitudes of a changing life in culture and environment. He had to cultivate his thinking faculties and devise a mode of travel that would relieve some of the monotonies of life such as a Crusoe sort and add to his ways of making a living for his family. He set up ship-building yards on the shores of the Pamlico Sound, designed and specialized in building two-masted schooners, small sail skiffs and fancy row boats. They constantly improved the beauty and serviceability of the schooner until the years between 1890 and 1905. During these years the magnificence of their ships reached a climactic finale.

Zion B. Scarborough built the schooner *Lonie Buren*, the most beautiful, graceful, and prideful ship that ever sailed the inland waters of North Carolina. Malachi Gray built the schooner *Thelma G*, a large two-masted schooner that served the wholesale merchants of Wilmington, N. C., in their trade with the large distributors of fancy groceries in Norfolk, Virginia. The traits of shipbuilding permeated the bloodstream of their hearts and souls, and is very much extant to this day.

Willie Austin, a native of Kinnakeet, is a shipbuilder and an inventive innovator of and designer of boats that are a credit to his ability and ingenuity to serve the ship-loving public. He inherited his capabilities of designing and building boats that meet the needs of a contemporary world from the Scarboroughs, Zion B. Scarborough and Lefficus Scarborough, the ancestors of his mother, Rosa Austin.

Willie has a small shipyard at modern Kinnakeet, and is overwhelmed with orders for boats from people all over the State of North Carolina and Virginia. He is a pleasant man and has a friendly personality, and will perhaps be the last shipbuilder of Kinnakeet.

When you come the Kinnakeet way, stop at Willie's shipyard and enjoy the personal friendliness of the Modern Kinnakeeter.

MODERN AVON

Willie Austin's shipyard. Tall man is Willie, talking to a prospective buyer. Willie's shipyard with a boat at the door. Two finished boats.

KINNAKEETER'S HOMECOMING

The Kinnakeeters are a group of families descended from a common ancestry of English and Indian by amalgamation, joined together by the same interest. It is an inherent tribal custom passed from generation to generation to be solicitous of each other's welfare by constant contact.

Their descendants meet yearly in a homecoming reunion, to keep their ancient fellowship and to keep their tribal loyalty in a united unbroken love. Their last homecoming was celebrated July 1, 1973.

I was selected to make the address of welcome to visiting Kinnakeeters and invited guests. The address evincing the feelings of the speaker and the visiting Kinnakeeters, is as follows:

Today I am speaking in behalf of the pastor, the official board, laymen, Sunday School Superintendent, teachers and entertainment management.

I wish to spread the red carpet of welcome to our fellow Kinnakeeters from all parts of the world, to our festive celebration of the word nearest to our hearts, homecoming. "Mid pleasures and palaces though we may roam, be it ever so humble, there is no place like home." The charm of home brings memories to us of Uncle Jesse's old ironbound wooden bucket that hung in his well. The pleasurable reminiscences of the joys of childhood, the swimming pool, the delicious crab roast, fishing with pin and string for mudfish in Uncle Riley's and Peters' ditch, our dolls, wearing our mothers' long dresses and high-heel shoes.

We welcome our guests who are participating with us on this festive occasion with a gratifying pleasure, and cordially extend the hand of fellowship. We extend to you cordial greetings of welcome and hope you will enjoy our hospitality, and tell the world about the friendly Kinnakeeter, who in the higher sensibilities of his soul loves his God, his neighbor, and God's people.

The joyous, happy, congenial faces of our many friends and visitors I see before me attests the feeling which this occasion has inspired in their hearts. These human faces glowing with love and joy from the impulse of a common gratitude which the blessings of fellowship warm their hearts. Our emotions are of happiness and joy.

We are in the church of our fathers and mothers. Our hearts turn reverently toward heaven in this beautiful temple of God, which has been blessed by their old-time religion, singing and shouting the songs of Zion and being merry men and women of God. We are in a church distinguished by their constancy and fidelity to the Rose of Sharon, the lily of the valley, the Morning Star of their hope and promise of eternal life by the spiritual Prince of their souls.

Most interesting to our hearts, feelings and affections is the heritage that we have been blessed with what makes this day of fellowship possible. We celebrate today the memory of our worthy ancestors and venerate their piety. We are proud to be the descendants of men and women who have set the world an example of raising their children in the nurture and admonition of the Lord, who left their children the heritage of honoring their father and mother, and teaching them that there is only one God, and to love the Lord their God with all their heart, mind and strength and their neighbor as their selves. A super heritage to venerate, to remember and love.

Today I am reminded of your sincere faith in God, which is a heritage handed down to you by the faith of your deceased fathers and mothers, with the fellowship that I have experienced with you. I am sure that your faith is strong and active, and alive today.

134

Today as I look out upon this congregation of pleasant people my heart is rent and torn asunder, and bleeding with anguish as I seek in vain to behold the cheerful and beautiful faces of my departed close neighbors, who have walked the last mile of the way. Our souls pleasantly look forward to the day when we will meet you just over the hilltop in the pearly white city of God that is soon coming down.

Our fathers and mothers who have departed this land of sorrow, and gone to the land of eternal life, are treasures of the familiar, a pleasant dream of love that has crossed the path of our lives.

In this assembly of happy, joyful humanity, my eyes search in vain for the faces of fathers and mothers, whatever their names, whether it be Austin, Brothers, Farrow, Miller, Meekins, O'Neal, Price, Quidley, Scarborough, or Williams, their seats are vacant. That is the sorrow and tragedy of our souls.

These saints have met their Pilot face to face and crossed the bar. Their Pilot has extended His hand and led them home.

We will always remember our departed fathers and mothers and keep them in sacred remembrance for the heritage that they have left us which makes this occasion possible.

My fellow Kinnakeeters, sons and daughters of these departed saints of glory, the precious memories that they have left us are glories to our soul.

Mr. J. B. Wright, in pleasant memory of his father and mother, has immortalized these memories for us in word and melody.

Precious memories, unseen angels, sent from somewhere to our soul,
How they linger, ever near us, and the sacred past unfold.
Precious father, loving mother, fly across the lonely years.
And old scenes of my childhood, in fond memory appear.
In the stillness of the midnight, echoes from the past I hear.

135

Old-time singing, gladness bringing, from that lonely
land somewhere.
As I travel on life's pathway, know not what the years
may hold.
Precious memories how they linger!

My fellow Kinnakeeters, as we reverence this precious
heritage, their living faith and precious memory today, let us
fellowship and love one another even as Christ has loved us.
When we partake of this food that God has so abundantly blessed us with for the sustenance of our physical bodies, let us
not forget the spiritual food that comes from the Creator's
storehouse, which is the food of fellowship, love, heritage,
faith and memory.

THE KINNAKEETER

A Poem

When the Kinnakeeter's last picture is painted
and his brushes have hardened, twisted and dried
and the beautiful colors have faded
and his good neighbors have died,
belief and faith he will need it,
and rest for an hour or two,
and his King of all good workman
will put him to work anew.
All Kinnakeeters will be happy.
They will sit in an Avon chair
and paint on rayon cloth
with brushes of white angora goat hair.
They will have saints to draw from—
John, Peter and Paul—
they will work all day busy
and never grow weary at all.
His King will praise him
and only his King will blame.
The Kinnakeeter will not work for presents or pay
and he will never work for fame.
And each for the pleasure of working
and for his separate star
the Kinnakeeter will paint things as he sees it
for the God of things as they are.
The Kinnakeeter will be joyful
and never utter a sigh
when his Prince,
the Boss of all good riders, passes by.

—Charles Williams II

THE FIRST LORDS PROPRIETORS' MAP OF CAROLINA
1672

We will use Roanoke Inlet the entrance to Roanoke Island as the pivotal cardinal point for the description of the map of the Sir Walter Raleigh Carolina Coastland. Beginning on the North side of Roanoke Inlet and extending northward to the Virginia State line. This land is known as the North Banks comprising the present villages of Nags Head, Colington, Kill Devil Hills, Kitty Hawk, Southern Shores and Corolla.

On Nags Head a few miles north of Roanoke Inlet is the Jockey Ridge sand dune formerly known in pre historic times as Kendricker Mount, the largest mountain of sand on the Atlantic side of the North American Continent. A magnificent silent sentry on duty awaiting to direct Sir Walter Raleigh's expedition to the historic Island of Roanoke.

On the South side of the inlet lies Hatteras Island the Hawaii of the Atlantic, an island of semitropical transcendent beauty the lost Eden of God.

The Kinnakeet Banks the paradise of the Atlantic, extending from Cape Hatteras northward to the present Oregon Inlet, comprising the villages of Kinnakeet, Scarborough Town, Little Kinnakeet, Clarks and Chicamacomico.

The South Banks, extends from Cape Hatteras to Hatteras Inlet, consisting of the villages of Hatteras, Trent, and the Cape of Hatteras now known as Buxton on Cape Hatteras.

The word Hatteras in Indian language means thin vegetation.

Hatteras Island in its primitive state was a land of luscious beauty, unspoiled by the destructive phenomena of the heavens above or the earth beneath.

139

Hatteras Island was inhabited by the Algonquin Indians for centuries, who roamed as kings and queens of this fairest portion of the earth, the most favored, happiest Indian of the North American Continent.

The Algonquin Indian in his hunt for food found Kinnakeet a fabulous bread basket, berries, fruits, figs, pears, apples, rabbit, opossum, racoon, deer, beach birds of every variety, willet curlew, sea chicken, snipe, rail, marsh hen, heron, egret, lark, robin, and during the winter season the skyway of travel from North Canada to Hatteras Island was teeming with millions of canada geese, brant, teal, white geese, red head, black head, canvas back and the elegant swan in super abundance.

In this eldorado of food wealth, the Indian was a gourmet of delicious fine foods, was joined by shipwrecked sailors who were cast ashore in vicious storms and made the Indians their people, and their God the Indians God. They came in increasing numbers and assimilated the Indians.

These sailors were English whom we attest by their names, Austins, Oden, Peeles, Styron, Gaskins, Ballances, Quidleys, Grays, Williams, Farrows, Stowes, Meekins, Caseys, Willis, Scarborough, Millers, Evans, Fosters, Morgans, Prices, O'Neals, Pughs, Hoopers, Smiths, Midgetts, Burrus, Barnetts, Jenettes and a host of others whose names are extant to this day.

Big Kinnakeet due to its geographical position in relation to Hatteras Island rapidly expanded and became the most populous, wealthiest and aggressive village on the coastal section of North Carolina.

Little Kinnakeet in integral part of Big Kinnakeet was sparsely settled. Scarborough Town was settled by one man, his name was Sylvester Scarborough. Mr. Scarborough was an adept suave trader and he set up a trading post at Scarborough Town and bartered traded with the people of Big Kinnakeet and Little Kinnakeet, he purchased the pelts of muskrats, otter, raccoon, skins of cattle and salt fish.

Scarborough used his sailing schooner and carried his pelts

to Washington, North Carolina, and bartered traded with the merchants in that city, and brought back to Scarborough Town, Porto Rico molasses, spices, black pepper, salt and medical supplies such as Balsam, Spirits Turpentine, British oil, laudanum, paregoric, Batemans drops, rum, gin, brandy, wine, cider and distilled strong liquors.

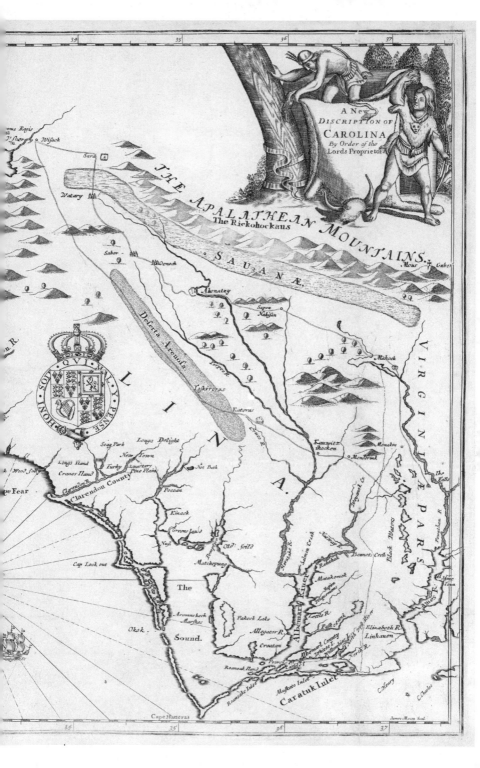

A New
DISCRIPTION OF
CAROLINA
By Order of the
Lords Proprietors

THE APALATHEAN MOUNTAINS.
The Rickohockaus
SAUANÆ

VIRGINIA PARS

Terra Regis
Wisack
Sara
Watary

Sahor
NWenock
Akenatzy
Sara
Nahisan
Toppos
Toskiroros
Katearas
Mahock
Maherinck
Rouakine
Kennitz hocken

Deserta Arenosa

Mons Guhen
The Falls

Longs Delight
Stag Park
New Town
Turky Quarters
Pine Plains
Hot Bath
Pocoan
Kinack
Greens Iland
Nuss
Old field
Matchepung

Wood folly
Woods Iland
Cranes Iland
Clarendon R.
Clarendon County

Cape Fear
Cap Look out

The

Okok

Sound.

Aromuskeck Marshes
Pakeck Lake
Allegator R.
Croatan
Roanoak Iland
Roanoak Inlet
Muscoto Inlet

Caratuk Inlet

Cape Hateras

Albemarl River
Paskotank R.
Matakomak
Vopim
Weapomeok
Little R.
Rakehok
Salmon Creek
Moratuc R.
Elizabeth R.
Linhauen
Bennets Creek
Black Water
Weyanock Cr.
Nansimon R.
Pomeork Cr.
James R.
C. Henry
C. Charles
Moor Town

James Moxon Sculp.